CHURCHILL
A VISUAL HISTORY

Published by IWM, Lambeth Road, London SE1 6HZ
iwm.org.uk

© The Trustees of the Imperial War Museum, 2024

All rights reserved. No part of this publication may be reproduced, stored in a retrieval system or transmitted, in any form or by any means, electronic, mechanical, photocopying, recording or otherwise without the prior permission of the copyright holder and publisher.

ISBN 978-1-912423-81-1

A catalogue record for this book is available from the British Library

Printed and bound by Gomer Press Limited
Colour reproduction by DL Imaging
Index by Susie Marques-Jones

All images IWM unless otherwise stated
Front cover: IWM COL 30
Back cover: IWM CAN 578

Every effort has been made to contact all copyright holders. The publishers will be glad to make good in future editions any error or omissions brought to their attention.

10 9 8 7 6 5 4 3 2 1

CHURCHILL
A VISUAL HISTORY

ANTHONY RICHARDS

CONTENTS

6   **INTRODUCTION**

12   **CHAPTER ONE**
EARLY LIFE

26   **CHAPTER TWO**
ENTERING POLITICS

38   **CHAPTER THREE**
THE FIRST WORLD WAR

62   **CHAPTER FOUR**
BETWEEN THE WARS

80   **CHAPTER FIVE**
WILDERNESS YEARS

92   **CHAPTER SIX**
FIGHTING ALONE

126 **CHAPTER SEVEN**
FIGHTING TOGETHER

150 **CHAPTER EIGHT**
THE PATH TO VICTORY

180 **CHAPTER NINE**
LIFE AFTER CONFLICT

196 **CHAPTER TEN**
CHURCHILL'S LEGACY

213   SOURCES
215   IMAGE LIST
217   ACKNOWLEDGEMENTS
219   INDEX

INTRODUCTION

In 2002, the BBC conducted a television poll to establish the *100 Greatest Britons*. At the top of the list, and therefore the person regarded by the viewing public at that time as the most important and influential British-born figure, was Winston Churchill.

Part of the reason for Churchill's high position in this and similar such surveys is surely his distinctive image (the hat, cigar and 'V' sign) and easily recognisable silhouette, which leads to the rare sort of instant recognition that is often reserved only for the most famous figures from history. Perhaps even more importantly, he benefits from an impressive reputation as one of the most prominent Allied leaders and the man who led Britain to victory during the Second World War. These factors alone are enough to make him both famous and fondly remembered. But his image and influence are even greater than that; to many minds he is also personally associated with the values which he instilled in the British population to urge them on during the war – the qualities of stoicism, integrity and strength – principles which the most patriotic might romantically suggest are inherently instilled within the very essence of being British.

But Churchill was a real person, and not a figure from historical fiction. Once we begin to examine his character, beliefs and actions in greater detail it becomes clear that the truth, as is always the case, is never so one dimensional.

For much of his life – and indeed one might say almost right up until the very moment that Britain declared war against Nazi Germany – Churchill was commonly regarded as both unreliable and self-aggrandising, known for being opinionated on all manner of subjects, whilst associated with some serious military failures and poor policy decisions. During the 1930s he was continually sidelined and eventually sent into the political wilderness, with many considering him a 'has been' politician who compared less favourably to his grander contemporaries who had reached the heights of Prime Minister, such as David Lloyd George or Herbert Asquith.

It would not be until the Second World War that circumstances made him the man we are so familiar with today. Many have argued that Churchill was the right person in the right place at the right time – the war leader that the country desperately needed to guide it towards an Allied victory over Nazi Germany. Success during that conflict and the resultant long-lasting boost to his reputation, not to mention his protracted life that ensured that he would be seen as the grand elder statesman, meant that he would continue to command respect both nationally and internationally long after the war was over.

In more recent years, however, Churchill has become a subject of criticism – for a number of valid reasons. Initially this disapproval centred around some of the political and military decisions he made throughout his career, most notably his attitude to Ireland; his reaction to the Bengal Famine; and his influence behind the Allied mass bombing campaign on German cities. Even during the war itself, some people retained a degree of suspicion regarding Churchill's aggression and potential selfishness, as recalled by wartime pacifist Leonard Clark:

OPPOSITE Copy after an original painting by Frank O Salisbury, 1943. Salisbury was one of the most successful portrait artists of his day, and painted many leading society figures from both sides of the Atlantic, including leading politicians and royalty. He is credited with having painted Churchill more often than any other artist.

I think most of what the Government put out sought to paint the other side in very lurid terms... this sort of Churchillian rhetoric was meant to be blood-curdling and I think we were mostly people who sort of felt that life wasn't as black and white as that... This was a great War Lord rather enjoying life.

More recently, criticism has tended to centre more on Churchill's personal character, with particular light being directed on the controversial statements he made on the subject of race. Most historians would accept that Churchill held hierarchical opinions on racial matters. At times he declared support for the racist conspiracy theory that atheistic Jewish revolutionaries were to blame for much of the world's social and political unrest, and also made disparaging remarks about Indians (especially Mohandas 'Mahatma' Gandhi, whom he loathed), Arabs and Chinese, all of whom he considered as inferior peoples.

While Churchill certainly declared beliefs that would not be considered remotely acceptable in today's society, we must remember the era in which he lived. Churchill was born and educated as a Victorian, and as such firmly believed in the popular view of the British Empire being superior and of immense importance to the development of the entire world. To Churchill and many others in that era, the British Empire was seen as a means of spreading Western civilisation and democracy across the globe – benefitting the inhabitants of Africa, India and elsewhere through education, rather than subjugation. Today we would regard such an argument as naively simplistic at best – or plainly untrue at worst – yet Churchill appears to have had a genuine, almost paternal, desire to protect and strengthen the British Empire, and much of his problematic statements might potentially be best viewed with this in mind. This is not to say that he should be completely forgiven for them, but we can go some way in understanding why he said these things and held such views.

It should also be said that Churchill's opinions on race could be nuanced. Although entertaining the idea of a 'revolutionary Jewish element', he was a strong supporter of Zionism. Indeed, both he and his father Randolph were regarded with suspicion by many of their Victorian contemporaries for often being *too* friendly with Jewish people. As early in his political career as 1906, Churchill also declared a firm support for the principle of equal civil rights, albeit in terms of the Empire being a protective parent:

La Corona branded cuban cigar, as smoked by Churchill and bought for him by his friend, the New York businessman Samuel Kaplan, in 1940. This particular stub was retained by one of Churchill's personal secretaries as a rather unique souvenir.

OPPOSITE TOP Lance Corporal Leigh of the Seaforth Highlanders carries his mascot, 'Churchill' the toy dog, during his wartime service. This photograph, taken in Italy on 7 February 1944, covers several of the Churchill tropes: bulldog, cigar and 'V' sign!

OPPOSITE BOTTOM Churchill's name was appropriated for numerous wartime vehicles and aircraft. Here the crew of 'Winnie', a Consolidated Liberator B Mark VI of No 159 Squadron RAF based at Digri, India, salute the nose insignia on their plane.

Such was the power of Churchill's speeches that memorable quotations from him would be regularly circulated throughout the war for propaganda purposes. This poster, promoting recruitment to the RAF, is one of the most famous examples from the Battle of Britain and references his speech of 20 August 1940 to the House of Commons.

> We will endeavour as far as we can to advance the principle of equal rights of civilised men irrespective of colour… We will not – at least I will pledge myself – hesitate to speak out when necessary if any plain case of cruelty or exploitation of the native for the sordid profit of the white man can be provided.

To Churchill, then, Britain and what he regarded as the virtues of the Empire were everything.

The manner in which Churchill has been regarded over time differs markedly between generations. Younger people today tend to see him in a much different light to those who lived through the war, no longer 'blinded' by his wartime reputation but rather regarding him in a more detached way as an historical personage, in the same way that one might think of Lord Nelson or Florence Nightingale. Churchill's instantly recognisable image lends itself to this, and his transformation from a real person to something approaching a fictional character has led to numerous portrayals in popular films and television series, ranging from the BBC's *Doctor Who* to Quentin Tarantino's *Inglourious Basterds*, all showing little regard to historical accuracy and often included purely for comedic value. In effect, Churchill's image and character has now almost become fictionalised in popular culture, divorced from historical reality. We all think we know how he looked and acted, what he believed in, and how he would react in any given situation. Today's culture dominated by social media only strengthens and promotes such largely uninformed views, with both praise and criticism often being heaped on Churchill's shoulders to push various personal or political agendas, often without recourse to corroborating evidence.

Churchill was by no means perfect and certainly far from the idealised role model which his status as 'Greatest Briton' surely suggests. But his remarkable character and determination, his impressive stamina for hard work, his skilled grasp of language and strong sense of humour are all indisputable. His influence on the course of world events throughout the twentieth century also cannot be denied, while it is his vital contribution to the Allied victory in the Second World War that will ensure that he is remembered as one of Britain's most important historical figures.

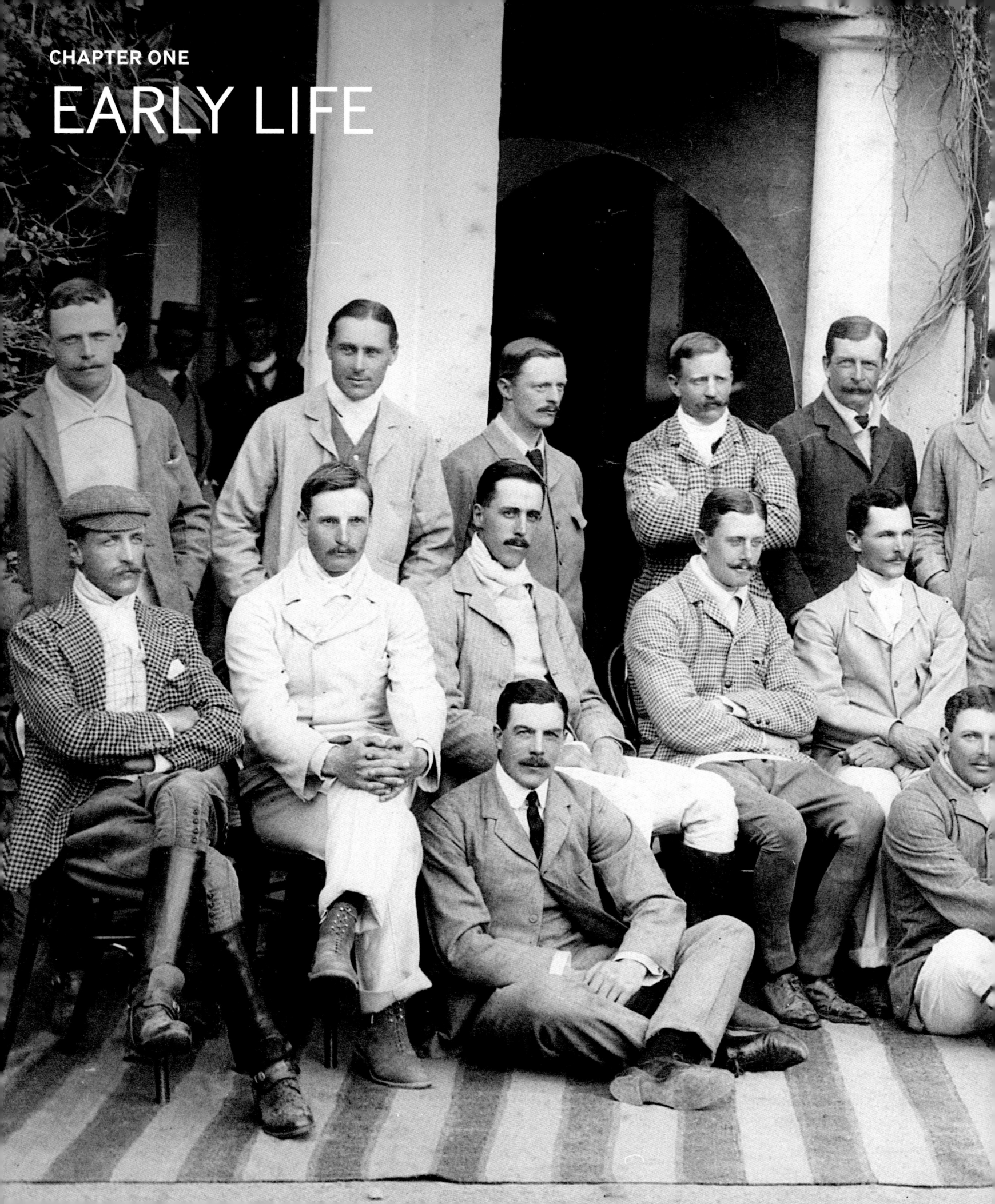

CHAPTER ONE

EARLY LIFE

Winston Churchill was born into the aristocracy on 30 November 1874, at his grandfather the Duke of Marlborough's ancestral family home of Blenheim Palace in Oxfordshire. Winston's father Randolph was an eminent Conservative politician who had married the wealthy American heiress Jennie Jerome the previous April, and while both parents would inevitably have an important influence on Winston's early life, he ended up spending much of his childhood in the care of others. The hectic social life enjoyed by both of his parents meant that they were often absent, making Churchill's upbringing largely the concern of his nanny and boarding schools. In this regard, Churchill was no different from many other children of the Victorian elite.

The young Winston's first experiences of education were not promising. He attended St George's Preparatory School in Ascot as a boarder from the age of seven, yet regular beatings from the headmaster led to his transfer to Brunswick School in Hove in 1884. For this he had his nanny, Elizabeth Everest, to thank, who was his closest friend and confidante and acted as a surrogate mother in Jennie Churchill's absence. Churchill's education at Hove was where he began to develop an avid love for reading, memorising long tracts of prose and poetry in a manner that would benefit him as a public speaker in later life.

Surviving correspondence reveals that while at Hove school Churchill wrote to his father expressing disappointment that he had not called to see his son when visiting the town. Indeed, the distance between the young Winston and his parents became even greater once the couple informally separated in 1886 when Churchill was just 11 years old. Although he was possibly unaware of the true situation, both his mother and father were somewhat notorious philanderers who had narrowly avoided a number of serious social scandals. In fact Randolph had already suffered from a very public spat with the Prince of Wales, which had led to his unofficial exile overseas for three years between 1877 and 1880 to serve as Private Secretary to his father, the Lord Lieutenant and Viceroy of Ireland. According to his later autobiography, Winston's earliest memories were of accompanying his grandfather to the unveiling of a statue in Ireland amid the military trappings of soldiers on horseback; as we shall see, these earliest memories perhaps influenced his lifelong obsession with soldiery.

At the age of 13 Winston narrowly passed the entrance exam for Harrow School and began his education there from April 1888. Expressing a certain disappointment in his son's intellectual capabilities, Randolph earmarked a military career for Winston and while at Harrow the young student began to attend the cadet training offered there. Churchill would later describe his time at Harrow as the worst five years of his life. He famously summarised his schooling by admitting that although he was always eager to learn, he did not necessarily appreciate being taught, and received regular beatings from his teachers as a result of his habitual disobedience.

On leaving Harrow, the natural path for a budding army officer

PREVIOUS PAGE Photograph showing the officers taking part in the Inter-Regimental Polo Tournament held at Meerut, in India, in 1899. Churchill (seen standing, second from right), who was serving with the 4th Hussars at the time, was already planning to enter politics and would stand for election back in Britain later that year — albeit unsuccessfully.

OPPOSITE Churchill as a young boy, aged 7, in Dublin c.1881. Winston's family had accompanied his grandfather, the Duke of Marlborough, to Ireland, where he was serving as Viceroy.

to follow was to apply to Sandhurst, the Royal Military College in Berkshire. Winston's first two applications were unsuccessful, but he was finally offered a place for the academic year beginning in September 1893. Churchill had displayed an interest in all things military from a very early age, in line with so many other young boys of that era. This fascination with soldiery was most clearly displayed through the large collection of toy soldiers that he amassed; by Churchill's own estimate, his assortment of troops amounted to nearly 1,500. Indeed, Churchill believed that his affection for the toy figures was one of the reasons that he embarked on an army career, as his father witnessed his fascination with all things military and proceeded to direct him accordingly. Having always enjoyed horse riding he chose to specialise in cavalry training at Sandhurst, to the annoyance of his father who would have preferred that his son pursue a more respected career in the Guards.

Churchill's first brush with politics occurred while at Sandhurst. He and his fellow cadets would make regular trips into London during their spare time to indulge in the myriad distractions that the capital city could offer. One of his favourite haunts was the Empire Theatre of Varieties in Leicester Square, which had become symbolic of the kind of degeneracy that social reformers were keen to eradicate. Many believed that the London theatres were becoming places of immorality, with the Empire's promenade in particular being a regular gathering place for prostitution and drunkenness. The local council's decision to renew the Empire's licence on the understanding that its promenade be obscured by screens and no alcohol sold in the auditorium, led to considerable public protest by regular theatregoers. Churchill joined the crowd in November 1894 who tore down the promenade barriers, and is reported to have delivered what was, in effect, a maiden public speech about the danger of government interference in people's social habits:

> Amid the cracking of timber and the tearing of canvas the barricades were demolished... In these somewhat unvirginal surroundings I now made my maiden speech. Mounting on the debris and indeed partially emerging from it, I addressed the tumultuous crowd. No very accurate report of my words has been preserved. They did not, however, fall unheeded, and I have heard about them several times since. I discarded the constitutional argument entirely and appealed directly to sentiment and even passion... These words were received with rapturous applause, and we all sallied out into the Square brandishing fragments of wood and canvas as trophies or symbols.

While Winston was beginning to develop a political conscience, by contrast his father's career in Westminster was already played out. Randolph had become Chancellor of the Exchequer in 1886 and it seemed would continue to hold high political office. Yet he was a wilful and opinionated individual, who commanded both respect and dislike in equal measure. After just five months in office as Chancellor, Randolph's over-confidence would lead to his downfall when he offered

OPPOSITE This portrait of Churchill was taken while he was attending Harrow public school in 1887.

EARLY LIFE 17

Jennie Churchill pictured with her son, now aged twenty, shortly after Lord Randolph's death in January 1895.

Lord Randolph Churchill, father to Winston and renowned Victorian politician.

the Prime Minister, Lord Salisbury, his resignation over the issue of military budgets. Despite having tried this tactic successfully on several previous occasions, this time Salisbury accepted the offer – and Randolph's political career was finished. Although he continued to sit in Parliament, his health rapidly declined (probably due to syphilis) and he died in January 1895 aged just 45, only a month after seeing his son pass out from Sandhurst as a cavalry officer.

Churchill would join his first regiment, the 4th Queen's Own Hussars, in February 1895. They were a well-known regiment, having taken part in the infamous Charge of the Light Brigade in the Crimean War just over forty years before. Always rather romantic in his outlook, Churchill would no doubt have found this link appealing, although over time he came to see his military career as essentially a stepping stone towards a different purpose – initially a career as a writer and journalist, but then increasingly as a politician, like his father before him.

Life at the Hussars' base in Aldershot was one full of routine and monotony, which was far from what Churchill wanted. He sought adventure and excitement, and during a short period of leave in October 1895 used his family connections to wangle a trip to Cuba, where the Spanish government was attempting to suppress a rebellion. Ostensibly being there in the capacity of a reporter for the *Daily Graphic* newspaper, he came under fire for the first time and used the opportunity to write florid accounts of the Cuban war for independence. His exhilaration in surviving the experience, not to mention the pay cheque received from the publication of his reports, led Churchill to pursue further opportunities as a war correspondent. Yet for now he was expected to follow the 4th Hussars to India, arriving in Bombay in October 1896. He was based in Bangalore for the following year and a half. Churchill coped with the largely uneventful routine of service life in India by reading voraciously, developing his knowledge of politics and indulging his love of horse riding, competing in races and winning trophies. He also grabbed any opportunity that he could for excitement, managing to join the Malakand Field Force in defending India's North-West Frontier, again notionally as an observer but in fact involved in a fighting capacity – in which he showed both bravery and recklessness. On his return to Bangalore in October 1897 he wrote what would become his first book, *The Story of the Malakand Field Force*. Receiving positive reviews, it spurred Churchill on to further writing opportunities.

With new journalistic endeavours in mind, he used his family connections and influence once again towards the end of 1898 to join Lord Kitchener's army, which was fighting to retake Sudan. Churchill was permitted by the War Office to join the expedition, but only at his own expense and risk. He therefore sought a temporary commission with the 21st Lancers, and again planned to use the opportunity to write eye-witness articles which he would sell to the *Morning Post* to finance his adventure.

Arriving in Cairo on 2 August 1898 and making his way down the Nile to Sudan, Churchill was present for the Battle of Omdurman on

LEFT 2nd Lieutenant Winston Churchill of the 4th Queen's Own Hussars, photographed shortly after joining his first regiment in February 1895. Some nine months later he would journey to Cuba to witness the attempted revolution.

BELOW British soldiers test a new Vickers Maxim machine gun in their camp during the Second Boer War. The introduction of such new weaponry sometimes conflicted with the need to rely on otherwise traditional fighting techniques, such as the use of cavalry.

Churchill's Webley Wilkinson M1892 pistol, carried during his military service in Cuba, India and Sudan. This weapon has a very unusual foresight fitted; the standard version is a large bead dovetailed into the barrel rib, but here, the foresight is a small bead let into a groove in the barrel rib and secured with a screw.

2 September. Notably, he would take part in the 21st Lancers' famous cavalry charge, which proved to be the final such large-scale attack by a British cavalry regiment. On reconnaissance with his unit near the city of Khartoum they spotted a few hundred enemy Sudanese troops, and the 400-strong 21st Lancers charged in to attack. But it turned out to be a trap, with the riders counter-attacked by a much larger force of enemy infantry. Fierce hand-to-hand fighting then ensued in which Churchill, commanding a small troop of Lancers, had to resort to using his automatic pistol to defend himself. He later considered the battle as having been perhaps the most dangerous moment of his entire life. The overall fight was a decisive one, however, and brought an end to the British campaigning to re-conquer Sudan. It was also the end of Churchill's formal military service, as he returned to India at the end of the year to resign his commission. Another book based on his experiences soon followed in 1899, *The River War: an Historical Account of the Reconquest of the Soudan*.

Churchill now decided that the time had come for him to enter the world of politics, and on returning to Britain in the summer of 1899 stood for election as one of the two Conservative candidates for Oldham in Greater Manchester. Although he lacked any particular connection to Oldham, Churchill's candidacy proved appealing to many because of his father's formidable political reputation. Despite this (and in spite of great confidence in his own candidacy), the by-election on 6 July went in favour of the Liberals and Churchill was defeated by some 1,500 votes. Part of the blame was undoubtedly due to the Conservative government's recent Clerical Tithes Bill which had raised local taxes to subsidise the Church and proved immensely popular with Oldham's largely nonconformist electorate, who voted accordingly. But despite this setback, Churchill remained convinced that the people of Oldham would welcome him as their representative if he could boost his personal popularity in some way – and a final military expedition might provide him with such an opportunity.

EARLY LIFE

The Second Boer War had just begun in South Africa in October 1899. Realising that this provided an opportunity not only to meet the demand back in Britain for eye-witness reportage of the conflict, but also to satisfy his own desire for dangerous adventure, Churchill journeyed to Cape Town as a journalist for the *Morning Post*. After just a few weeks, he was in the midst of the fighting. On 15 November Churchill found himself travelling in an armoured train as part of a scouting expedition inside the British Natal Colony. An ambush by the Boers resulted in the train being partially derailed, leaving the British troops surrounded and besieged. Churchill led efforts to get the train operational again and it finally escaped, but leaving him behind with a small group of British soldiers who were all taken prisoner. Although Churchill was there as a civilian war correspondent, he was in uniform and allegedly armed, which meant that he was immediately treated as a prisoner of war. Recognised by the Boers, he was also seen as a potentially valuable bargaining piece.

The British prisoners were transported to Pretoria and imprisoned in a converted schoolhouse, where Churchill immediately started to plan an escape. He concentrated on studying the routine of the guards in order to spot an opportunity to flee, and did so on the night of 12 December by climbing a ten-foot wall around the prison. Having quickly seized the sudden chance to escape, he left behind the two fellow officers who were intending to accompany him; as these other men were carrying the escape equipment (including a map, compass and rations) which were essential for survival during the 300-mile journey to freedom, Churchill now faced significant problems:

> I was in the heart of the enemy's country. I knew no one to whom I could apply for succour. Nearly three hundred miles stretched between me and Delagoa Bay. My escape must be known at dawn. Pursuit would be immediate. Yet all exits were barred. The town was picketed, the country was patrolled, the trains were searched, the line was guarded... Worst of all, I could not speak a word of Dutch or Kaffir, and how was I to get food or direction? But when hope had departed, fear had gone as well.

Undaunted, Churchill set off as a hunted fugitive and began to walk towards Portuguese East Africa, unaware that the Boers were appealing for his recapture with a bounty of £25, either dead or alive.

Briefly hitching a ride on a freight train, Churchill had to resort to walking for many miles through the wilderness. As his hunger and thirst grew worse, he realised that he would have to seek help but by great fortune the first person he met happened to be one of the few sympathetic Englishmen in the Transvaal region. John Howard was a colliery manager, and together with another Briton named Dan Dewsnap, the fugitive was sheltered in their mine until a plan could be made to get him to safe territory. Churchill was eventually hidden amongst sacks loaded onto a train for Portuguese East Africa, arriving there on 21 December and marking an end to his traumatic adventure.

As a war correspondent for the *Morning Post*, Churchill was captured by the Boers while travelling in an armoured train which was wrecked. This photograph depicts the group of British soldier prisoners, with Churchill standing apart on the right.

EARLY LIFE 23

Never the sort of person to voluntarily rest, Churchill was soon back to witness not only the Battle of Spion Kop on 23 January 1900, but also the final relief of the besieged Ladysmith in February.

Press coverage of Churchill's experiences in the Boer War made him a celebrity back home. The accounts of his experiences as a fugitive were avidly read by the British public, and on his return to Britain in July 1900 he received a hero's welcome, with Oldham alone greeting him with great crowds and a brass band. By immense good fortune, his links with the town had been strengthened by the fact that one of his South African rescuers had originated from there. This huge boost to Churchill's reputation would improve his standing in the imminent General Election scheduled for 1 October 1900, for which his mother had already been working hard to drum up support. During Randolph's lifetime, Jennie had embraced the political arena and encouraged her husband's ambitions; her intelligence and popularity in Victorian society ensured that she remained a widely admired and influential person. Following her husband's early death, Jennie now focused her support on Winston. It was therefore she more than anybody else who worked so hard to build Churchill's reputation as a young politician, raising financial support and encouraging press interest.

It was almost exactly a year since his first electoral defeat, yet on this occasion Churchill's reputation had preceded him. While the Liberals once again retained an overall electoral majority in Oldham, it was not enough to stop Churchill from being successfully elected as Oldham's second MP, representing the Conservative Party. The next important stage in his life was about to begin.

Perhaps memories of Churchill's brief time as a prisoner of war in Boer hands influenced British prisoners of war held in Stalag XX-A in Thorn, Poland, during the Second World War. They added grafitti to the walls of their cell blocks, and here a prisoner has scrawled a message to Churchill, entreating him to 'give the German B[astard]s hell'.

CHAPTER TWO
ENTERING POLITICS

Churchill's election at Oldham would mark the beginning of his exceptionally long career as a Member of Parliament. However, as MPs did not receive a salary in this era, the need to earn money became a matter of urgency for the young politician. Having just published a book of his South African experiences to capitalise on his new-found fame, Churchill decided that the quickest and simplest means to boost his income further before taking up his parliamentary seat in February 1901 would be a lecture tour. By continuing to make money through writing and journalism while running a parallel career as a politician, Churchill was only emulating his late father Randolph, who himself had written extensively to fund his aristocratic lifestyle.

The lecture tour began on 26 October 1900 at Harrow School, where Churchill had boarded less than a decade before, to be followed by a circuit of the country before embarking for North America in December. Newspaper reviews of his talks were unanimously positive, yet unfortunately for Churchill, the American part of the tour did not prove to be quite as successful, as he later recalled in his memoirs.

> A different atmosphere prevailed in the United States. I was surprised to find that many of these amiable and hospitable Americans who spoke the same language and seemed in essentials very like ourselves, were not nearly so excited about the South African War as we were at home. Moreover a great many of them thought the Boers were in the right; and the Irish everywhere showed themselves actively hostile.

It also didn't help that he fell out with Major James Pond, his US agent, after being forced to speak to several near-empty houses. But the North American tour *did* provide an opportunity for Churchill to mix with the elite of American society which included the author Mark Twain, US President William McKinley and the future President Theodore Roosevelt. He also remained buoyant over his earnings from the British leg of the lecture tour, and subsequent dates in Paris, Madrid and Gibraltar brought the trip to a successful conclusion. Fully appreciative of the considerable amount of money he had made in a relatively short space of time, Churchill would undertake similar lecture tours on many future occasions throughout his life, especially to North America where he would be regularly welcomed much more positively in later years.

Churchill finally took up his seat in the House of Commons on 14 February 1901, as the Conservative MP for Oldham. At first he seemed to be emulating his late father's political stance, which although remaining Tory in outlook included support for more radical social policies. He also shared a lot of his father's independent nature; defending Conservative policy when required, he was also quick to put his own personal beliefs above the party line. This led to Churchill beginning to distance himself more and more from the Tory government on a number of issues, but especially the treatment of the Boers in South Africa. Although having taken up arms (albeit

PREVIOUS PAGE Christabel Pankhurst speaks at a rally in Trafalgar Square, London in 1908. Christabel and her mother Emmeline founded the Women's Social and Political Union (WSPU) in Manchester in 1903, which used militant campaigning in an attempt to gain women the vote. Churchill was hesitant in fully supporting the principle of extending the vote, and as such became a target for many suffragettes.

OPPOSITE A half length photographic portrait of Winston Churchill taken in 1900, the year he was elected as a Conservative Member of Parliament for Oldham.

unofficially) against them and been treated as a captive in their hands, he now supported their political rights. But more than anything else, it was the subject of Free Trade which would come to swing the opinion of both he and others against the government. The Conservatives were adhering to a protectionist trade policy, while Churchill and others felt that economic prosperity would be more likely if a tariff-free, Free Trade strategy was adopted instead.

This disagreement came to a head on 31 May 1904, when Churchill dramatically 'crossed the floor' of the House of Commons to switch allegiance and sit on the opposition Liberal benches. Although the Free Trade debate was the catalyst for this political switch, Churchill would also come to wholeheartedly embrace the social policies of the Liberal Party. The Conservative Prime Minister, Arthur Balfour, lost a major Commons vote in July 1905 but refused to stand down until 4 December, when the Liberals were asked to form a new, minority government under their leader Sir Henry Campbell-Bannerman. The Liberals proceeded to win a landslide victory at the polls in January 1906, with Churchill winning the seat for Manchester North-West. That month would prove a significant one for Churchill; not only did his biography *Lord Randolph Churchill* see print, but the first biography written about Winston himself had also just appeared, confirming that the son was beginning to generate as much interest as his late father.

Churchill was now offered a senior post in the new Liberal government as Financial Secretary to the Treasury, but turned it down in favour of the less-important yet highly influential Under-Secretary of State for the Colonies. Working with the Colonial Secretary Lord Elgin, Churchill did much towards resolving the situation with the Boers in South Africa, drafting a constitution for the Transvaal and helping South Africa to gain independence and dominion status which would come to pass in 1910.

Campbell-Bannerman's ill health meant that Herbert Asquith took over as Prime Minister in April 1908, and at the age of only 33, Churchill was appointed to the Cabinet as President of the Board of Trade. However, he was fated to lose his seat at the by-election that same month and had to stand again on 9 May for the safe Liberal seat of Dundee, which he won comfortably.

1908 would prove to be an important year for Churchill. Not only did he become a Cabinet minister for the first time, but he got married on 12 September to the woman who would henceforth become his closest companion for the remainder of his long life. Winston had first met Clementine Hozier some four years before at a ball organised by the Earl and Countess of Crewe, yet had only begun courting her in a serious manner from the spring of 1908. Ever the romantic, he proposed to her in the Temple of Diana located in the grounds of Blenheim Palace. Clementine (or Clemmie, as he affectionately called her) would remain at Churchill's side throughout the years to come, supporting him through the stresses and strains of high office and two world wars. Setting up home at a house in Eccleston Square in London,

RIGHT This photographic portrait of Churchill was taken in 1904, the year in which he would 'cross the floor' to change parties, joining the Liberals in support of their Free Trade policies. He would eventually return to the Conservative Party in 1924.

BELOW A portrait of Clementine Hozier and her fiancé Winston Churchill, taken to mark the occasion of their engagement in 1908.

A crowd of women listen to a speech by a women's rights activist, in a photograph likely to have been taken during the period that Churchill was Chancellor of the Exchequer. Giving women the right to vote was one of the greatest political issues facing the country at the turn of the century.

near enough for Winston to easily reach Westminster, the couples' first daughter Diana was born in July 1909.

Together with David Lloyd George, the Chancellor of the Exchequer who would become Prime Minister in 1916, Churchill spent much of the next few years in Cabinet pushing through government policies that resulted in important social reforms. Basic social rights such as a living wage, state-funded unemployment insurance and labour exchanges were all introduced by the Liberal government through the hard work of both Churchill and Lloyd George. One of the reforms with which Churchill became most associated during this era of change was his reform of the House of Lords. In 1907 he drew attention to its ability to obstruct an elected government's policies at will, and subsequent restructuring not only served to reduce the size of the house, but also to curb its power.

Such reforms did, of course, affect his popularity in certain social circles. Churchill's criticism of Balfour and his 'turncoat' defection to the Liberals made him somewhat of a pariah amongst Conservatives and allegedly attracted the disgust of the King himself. A number of Tory clubs rescinded his membership, forcing him to create his own unofficial 'Other Club' in 1906, which met at regular intervals at the Savoy Hotel in London and was comprised of close friends and fellow politicians – even from the Opposition.

Following a General Election which resulted in a narrow Liberal win, Churchill was promoted to Home Secretary in February 1910. One of the major domestic issues at that time was the question of women's suffrage. The idea of giving women the right to vote had been widely opposed in Victorian Britain, with many from both genders (including Churchill himself) believing that women's political views should be represented by their husband's vote. Politics was commonly viewed as a rowdy male pastime, in which women should not concern themselves. But as government involvement in everyday life increased through the Liberal government's social reforming, public opinion began to change. Churchill's views adapted too, undoubtedly influenced by Clementine who was an ardent supporter of women's suffrage. He therefore came to support the principle of votes for women, although only if the majority of the existing male electorate agreed, through a referendum. Many others, including the Prime Minister Herbert Asquith, remained ardently opposed. Suffragists were unhappy with Churchill's lack of a more strident support for their cause and, indeed, his attitude would waver in the face of the social discontent that their more militant members were now causing, through the disruption of parliamentary debates and various criminal acts.

Britain was also faced with civil unrest during this period from striking coal miners protesting against low wages and poor working conditions. The Tonypandy riots during the summer months of 1910 saw Churchill order several hundred London police officers to Wales to assist their local colleagues in keeping the peace, while soldiers were also partially deployed in readiness. This decision caused many to regard Churchill as being heavy-handed in dealing with the situation, with the recently formed Labour Party portraying him as an opponent of workers' rights, despite the fact that he believed that the mine owners were acting unreasonably.

Another key moment during Churchill's time as Home Secretary was his involvement in the Siege of Sidney Street. London's East End at that time was characterised by destitution and over-crowding which, combined with the presence of socialist revolutionaries and gang culture, led to violence erupting in the area on a regular basis. For any Home Secretary, the East End was therefore a danger zone which needed to be watched very carefully. Since the beginning of 1909, one particular gang of Russian Latvian revolutionaries had committed a series of robberies which became something of a sensation. Their latest plan to rob a jeweller's shop by tunnelling through from an adjacent property was thwarted on 16 December 1910, leading to a street battle in which three unarmed policemen were killed. A manhunt began for the criminal gang, and after a few days the police learned that two members were hiding at a property on Sidney Street in East London.

With Churchill's agreement as Home Secretary, armed police and soldiers besieged the house on 3 January 1911. The criminals refused to surrender and calls for reinforcements reached Churchill, who rushed to the scene himself, conspicuous in his astrakhan collared coat and top hat. As the most prominent figure of authority on the scene, Churchill encouraged calls for artillery to support a storming of the house, while also suggesting that metal shields be obtained to allow police to safely approach the property. But before any such ideas could be put into proper operation, a fire unexpectedly broke out on the upper floor of the building and began to spread. The Fire Brigade arrived but Churchill stepped in, with the support of the police, to stop them extinguishing the flames in the hope that the blaze might encourage the criminals to surrender. However the fire got out of control and the gang members were later found burned to death inside; several firemen were also hurt during the blaze, with one of them dying from his injuries some months later.

Afterwards, Churchill was criticised for attending the siege in so public a manner, with his opponents accusing him of using the incident for self-publicity. Writing about the incident some years later, he came to accept that such criticisms were perhaps 'not altogether unjust':

> Party controversy was then at its height in England, and I was much criticized in the newspapers and in Parliament for my share in this curious episode. Mr Balfour in the House of Commons was especially sarcastic. 'We are concerned to observe,' he said in solemn tones, 'photographs in the illustrated newspapers of the Home Secretary in the danger zone. I understand what the photographer was doing, but why the Home Secretary?'

Bearing in mind Churchill's character as somebody always keen to be wherever the action was, as shown by his numerous military excursions as a young man, in all likelihood he simply wanted to

witness the situation first-hand. In doing so, he would be trying to satisfy the same impulse which years later would see him try to attend the D-Day landings. The political aftermath of Sidney Street saw increasing demands for stronger immigration laws, with Churchill himself proposing, albeit unsuccessfully, a harsh Aliens (Prevention of Crime) Bill directed against 'unassimilated foreigners'.

Churchill's time as Home Secretary seems to have instigated a change in his political views, with his original radicalism now moving in a more noticeably Conservative right-wing direction. Perhaps he recognised a need for harsher policies to counter the social disorder with which he was tasked with dealing. Following the Tonypandy riots, further strikes and civil unrest throughout 1911 saw him order troops to quell dock workers protesting in Liverpool, as well as a national railway worker strike that same year. It was therefore perhaps with a sense of relief that Churchill switched roles in October 1911 to become First Lord of the Admiralty. This new role would allow Churchill to make his mark in an even greater way, especially as a major conflict approached.

OPPOSITE The Siege of Sidney Street, 2 January 1911. Armed anarchists barricaded themselves inside the property and fired at police and soldiers of the 1st Battalion Scots Guards, before the house was set on fire. Churchill was present throughout.

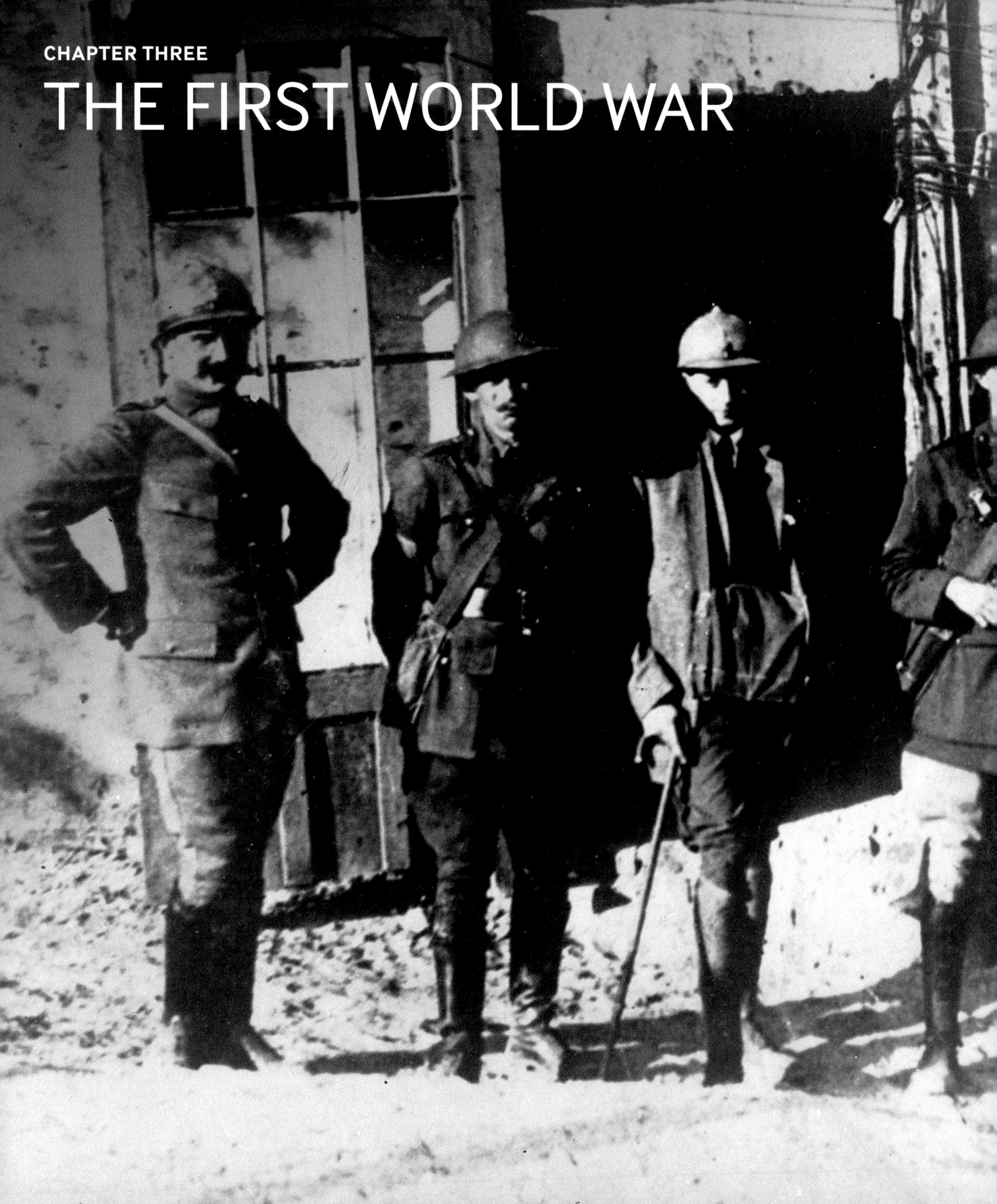

CHAPTER THREE
THE FIRST WORLD WAR

As First Lord of the Admiralty, Churchill was now the political head of the Royal Navy and the government's senior adviser on all naval matters. In an era in which Britain's Navy remained the most powerful such force in the world, protecting the far flung reaches of the British Empire as well as the United Kingdom itself, the role was an exceptionally important one.

Within a matter of days of his appointment in October 1911, Churchill issued a Cabinet memorandum calling for the establishment of a special naval staff in preparation for a likely European conflict. The rate at which the German Navy was increasing in size and strength was proving a serious concern to many including Churchill, as it presented a clear threat to international security. For his next two and a half years in the post, Churchill therefore made naval improvements his overwhelming priority. He visited hundreds of naval stations, dockyards and ships and developed an understanding of naval tactics and gunnery skills, all in an attempt to ensure that Britain stayed ahead of Germany's ever-advanced naval construction. Taking full advantage of the official Admiralty yacht HMS *Enchantress*, Churchill visited far and wide to make regular inspections of ships and facilities, as Gilbert Adshead recalled from his service as an Artificer in the battleship HMS *Lord Nelson*:

> He was very well liked in the Navy because he was approachable and he liked to find out for himself. Now on one occasion when we were at Sheerness lying at the No 1 buoy, one Sunday morning somewhere about twenty to eight, when the ship was at breakfast and everybody was getting ready to dress in their number ones for division and divine service and so on, the officers as well, there was a long shoreman's pulling boat, a rowing boat, came alongside the officer gangway on the quarter deck. And a figure walked up wearing a cloak, walked up onto the quarter deck, raised his hat to the quarter deck because you always had to salute the quarter deck when you came onboard. This civilian figure raised his hat to the quarter deck and of course the quartermaster immediately legged it straight over and said 'What the devil do you want?' And he said 'That's alright my man, don't you worry, I'm the First Lord of the Admiralty'. 'Oh, I'll go and tell the officer on watch', and he said, 'You'll do no such thing, you'll tell nobody. I'm going for'ard to have a look round... I know my way round, there's no need for you to worry. Carry on with your duty, I'm going for'ard'.
>
> Now he... roamed all the mess decks, many of them were having breakfast and he talked to everybody, he poked his head inside the officers' mess and had a talk with us. Of course as soon as he'd gone the quartermaster legged it to the officer of the watch... he told the commanding officer, he told everybody off, and all the officers came bustling along pulling on their jackets, traipsing after Winston Churchill. And he just turned round and said, 'Gentlemen, please don't disturb yourself, I know you're very busy getting ready for divisions and divine service, carry on with your normal duties, I'm only

PREVIOUS PAGE Churchill stands alongside officers of the 29th French Division at Nieuport, Belgium, during his military service on the Western Front in the First World War, February 1916.

OPPOSITE This wooden figure of Churchill, portrayed here as 'Britannia', was built by the Lord Roberts Memorial Workshop and sold for charity during the First World War. The figure formed part of a series called 'Men Who Matter', and was likely to have been commissioned before Churchill's fall from grace after the Dardanelles affair of 1915.

Churchill, as First Lord of the Admiralty, sits in a Short-Sommer Pusher Biplane T2 of the Royal Flying Corps (Naval Wing), while learning to fly at Eastchurch, Kent in 1913. In the foreground (facing left) is Lieutenant Gilbert Wildman-Lushington, Churchill's favourite instructor, who was killed in a flying accident the month after this photograph was taken.

having a look round.' And the commander said, 'Oh well sir, I'll away the picket boat to get you to shore again.' He said, 'No you won't, I've got my own boat lying off there' – a rotten old rowing boat. And he rowed ashore!

Churchill was also keen to ensure that new naval recruits were being trained in the appropriate way, with visits to shore establishments such as HMS *Ganges* at Shotley being a regular thing, as boy seaman Albert Masters later recalled:

> He came to Harwich, oh I don't suppose I'd been there a fortnight, when much to our amazement the First Lord was coming. Well that didn't mean anything to us, we damn soon learned who it was though because the *Enchantress* tied up to one of the buoys in Harwich and he came round and I can still see him now in my mind's eye. He was at that time of day in a grey suit with grey topper... and he used to make a point, he would not only interview the officer... but he had no compunction to go to a boy and saying, 'Are you quite happy, is there anything wrong?' In other words it was a personal affair, and I met him many times afterwards and he never altered. He was very greatly respected in the Navy.

Such visits did much to inform Churchill's knowledge. To prepare the fleet for a potential war, the Royal Navy's ships were converted to more efficient oil-fired engines while training exercises were increased. He also made efforts to invite Germany to join with Britain in a mutual de-escalation of naval construction, yet without success.

These concerns for a European war with Germany were realised in 1914, when the political and military alliances between nations drew Britain into what would become a major conflict, beginning in Europe but spreading globally. Overseeing the nation's naval war effort, Churchill continued to push for greater expenditure, highlighting the importance of new technology in fighting the war such as submarines (which Germany would use to great effect in their attempts to restrict shipping and isolate Britain) and aircraft (through the Royal Naval Air Service, formally created in July 1914). As the fighting developed, he would also call for greater mechanisation on the Western Front and pushed the idea of armoured tanks on caterpillar tracks, creating an Admiralty Landships Committee in February 1915 to encourage developments.

Early military effort in the war was directed towards stopping the German advance into France and Belgium, in the months before trench warfare became an indication that a stalemate had set in. Always one to involve himself in the midst of any action, Churchill visited Antwerp in October 1914 and witnessed how the Belgian troops were struggling to defend the town against German attack. He promised British reinforcements, which subsequently appeared in the form of the Royal Naval Division (RND), made up from 'spare' volunteers and reservists from the Royal Navy who operated as land-based infantry.

However, the RND were not enough to stop Antwerp falling into German occupation, and many of their number ended up as prisoners, spending the rest of the war interned in Groningen camp in the Netherlands. Criticised for going to Antwerp personally and initiating what many regarded as a somewhat ill-thought out course of action, Churchill insisted that the RND's stance at Antwerp had allowed other locations, such as the ports of Calais and Dunkirk, to remain in Allied hands. Norman Macleod was private secretary to George Lambert MP, the Civil Lord of the Admiralty, and recorded his observations on Churchill's character at that time:

> In his Naval Division scheme he has shown his weaknesses – his mind works quickly, is fertile in suggestions and he is a tremendous worker, but he lacks balance and consistency [and] does not work well in harness – I cannot imagine him conceiving a great scheme and carrying it through steadily. He begins no end of things, threatens Heads of Departments with dire penalties if his plans are not carried out – then falters and delays giving a decision and then drops the scheme.

Frustrated with the deadlock which had by now established itself on the Western Front, Churchill began to look further afield for a way in which to steer the course of the war in a manner more favourable to Britain's interests. The Middle East was one theatre of war which might serve such a purpose. The Ottoman Empire had just entered the war in support of Germany, but if Turkey could be removed from the conflict, then this might serve to weaken its partner while providing strategic benefits to Britain and its allies. Particular attention was drawn to the Dardanelles, a narrow strip of water in north-western Turkey which divided Europe from Asia and remained of particular strategic significance. Once Turkey had entered the war, the Dardanelles had been effectively closed off in order to prevent access to the Sea of Marmara. The opening of a new front via the Dardanelles therefore now presented itself as an attractive new strategy for the British and French.

Churchill pushed for an attack by ships alone in order to force the Dardanelles and provide access to Constantinople, yet such a plan would only work if the Turkish defences could be easily destroyed. British and French ships began a naval assault on 19 February 1915 which proved unsuccessful; Turkish guns on both sides of the Dardanelles and extensive minefields prevented any headway being made. The answer was for French and British troops (and in particular soldiers from the Empire including Australians, New Zealanders and Indians) to stage an amphibious assault on the Gallipoli peninsula beginning on 25 April. This operation proved difficult and costly, and despite a fresh assault in August the Turks managed to hold back the invaders, meaning that the campaign would finally be abandoned in January 1916. It had been an utter failure on almost every level, with total casualties from both sides reaching a figure of well over half a million.

PREVIOUS PAGE *The Base Camp, Cape Helles, Under Shell Fire, August 1915* by Norman Wilkinson. In this painting several troopships in the Dardanelles come under fire from the shore, while to the left of the painting, the converted collier *River Clyde* has been run aground during the landing of troops and lists to one side.

Churchill was the chief instigator of the Dardanelles campaign, and as one of the key members of the committee which had overseen its direction was held personally responsible for the campaign's failure. Criticism of his rash decision-making had started early on when the initial naval attempt to force the Dardanelles had failed, and had reached a point in May shortly after the landings on Gallipoli when he was effectively sacked as First Lord of the Admiralty by Prime Minister Herbert Asquith. Churchill's removal was a necessary condition imposed by the Conservatives before they would support Asquith's new wartime Coalition government, although Churchill's increasing disparity with the views of the First Sea Lord, Lord Fisher, were already forming such a tense atmosphere that the two men could no longer work together. Churchill would remain in the Coalition Cabinet as the more junior Chancellor of the Duchy of Lancaster.

As his relationship with Asquith swiftly deteriorated, Churchill realised that the Prime Minister and many of the (largely Conservative-controlled) newspapers were portraying him as a scapegoat for the Dardanelles failure. Trying desperately but failing to secure the release of government papers which he believed would vindicate him from blame, Churchill resigned from the government on 25 November 1915. The following year would see a Commission of Enquiry into the Dardanelles affair, but until then Churchill would decide to take out his frustrations on the enemy in a more personal way, by resuming his army commission as an infantry officer in the trenches.

Embarking for the Western Front in November 1915, Churchill was initially attached to the Grenadier Guards in order to gain first-hand experience of the trenches. While others in his position may have chosen the much safer option of taking a staff position away from the front line, Churchill characteristically preferred to embrace danger. Before too long, in January 1916 he was promoted to Lieutenant Colonel of the 6th Battalion Royal Scots Fusiliers. The next few months would see Churchill and his men under regular artillery bombardment, facing all the usual dangers of trench life including snipers and machine gun fire, with the only factor in their favour being the fact that they were stationed near Ploegsteert, a part of the line in Flanders with a reputation for being relatively safe compared to most other sectors. Also, Churchill was fortunate to be in the trenches at a time when there were no major offensives planned by either side.

Although very real danger certainly remained, Churchill failed to show any particular concerns over his own safety and did not appear to be overly bothered about the discomfort of trench life. Indeed, his privileged existence followed him to the trenches, since amongst the equipment which accompanied him everywhere was a portable tin bath and hot water tank. He also benefitted from Clementine back home, who would send regular hampers of food and alcohol which made his time on the Western Front far more palatable. Even when the supplies from home ran dry, he was able to charm the locals into helping to feed him; on the occasion that his battalion commandeered a hospice run by Belgian nuns, Churchill successfully persuaded the sisters to prepare

ABOVE This Colt Government model (M1911) pistol was purchased by Churchill in 1915. He carried it while serving on the Western Front as commanding officer of the 6th Battalion Royal Scots Fusiliers during the first half of 1916. Reputed to be one of his favourite guns, it bears obvious signs of frequent use, and has his name engraved along one side.

OPPOSITE The 21st Australian Infantry Battalion march up Monash Gully after arriving at Gallipoli, April 1915. Churchill would forever be associated with the campaign, which resulted in high casualty rates and no military advantage.

Churchill, as the British Minister of Munitions, is pictured alongside Lord Northcliffe (Alfred Harmsworth) at the French Foreign Office in Paris, 29 November 1917. Northcliffe was a newspaper magnate who acted as director of propaganda for the Lloyd George government.

soup and other meals for himself and his fellow officers.

Churchill's reputation amongst his men was mixed. On the one hand he was a conscientious officer, looking after their health and safety as far as he was able. Yet at the same time he generated frustration amongst them by directing his men in the core duties of trench construction and making regular impractical suggestions on how to 'improve' their situation, such as ordering artillery bombardments for no obvious advantage. Indeed, Lieutenant Colonel C E L Lyne, an officer in the Royal Field Artillery who was also serving on the Western Front at that time, recalled how Churchill's encouragement of aggression towards the enemy only served to make the sector more dangerous – he 'stirred things up so much that the rest of the civilians were evacuated about this time'. But while Churchill could be a strict disciplinarian by expecting his men to meet his own high standards, he was also generous, allowing fellow officers to use his tin bath and keeping everybody entertained with his good humour during meal times.

General Sir Ivo Vesey recalled an encounter which indicates Churchill's frustrations at having much reduced military influence at this time:

> He walked into my office one day, he was then commanding a battalion of I think the Royal Scots Fusiliers, he was up in the front line, in the trenches there... He'd been removed from his post at the First World War Admiralty by Asquith and then he'd volunteered to come out to France which accounted for his presence in my office that morning. When he came in, and after a short talk with me... he then disclosed what was the real object of his visit. He asked me if I thought there was any chance of his being promoted to command a brigade. Well, I said I really didn't know, it depended entirely on the recommendation of his brigade and divisional commanders. Well, then I took him off to lunch. I particularly remember that meeting because of a remark he made to me as he was leaving. He said: 'I'm never going to have anything more to do with politics and politicians. When this war is over I shall confine my activities entirely to writing and painting.' Fortunately his forecast wasn't a particularly accurate one!

More than anything else, Churchill used his time on the Western Front to lead by example, often undertaking risky reconnaissance missions into No Man's Land under the cover of darkness. He brushed with death several times, once witnessing shrapnel narrowly miss him during a visit from his cousin the Duke of Marlborough. On another occasion he was called to meet a car behind the lines which would take him to a staff meeting. But after an hour's walk trudging through mud under fire, he came to find that the vehicle had turned back due to shelling. Churchill returned angrily to his dugout, only to find it in ruins – it had received a direct shell hit while he was away, killing one of his fellow officers.

Despite the opportunities for excitement provided to Churchill in

NEXT PAGE Major Winston Churchill, wearing a French steel helmet, photographed at the headquarters of XXXIII Corps, French Army, at Camblain L'Abbé while visiting the French front line on 15 December 1915.

the trenches, he remained a Member of Parliament and still aspired to return full time to politics. When returning to London on leave, he had taken the opportunity to speak in the Commons which, although badly received due to the reputational damage from which he was still suffering as a result of the Dardanelles, did serve to remind people of his continued political presence. But at any rate Churchill's military service was not to last, for in May 1916 he requested permission to rescind his commission and return to civilian life once more. His time would now chiefly be occupied by politics, although the spectre of the Dardanelles remained to haunt him.

Churchill's calls for a proper Commission of Enquiry into the Dardanelles affair were finally realised in July 1916, and he gave evidence to the committee in September of that year while doing his best to encourage others to step forward in his support. The preliminary findings of the Commission were released in a First Report of March 1917. Their conclusion presented few surprises, with the main finding being that the Dardanelles campaign had been both badly planned and poorly executed, with too little consideration given to the many problems it would face. Practical supply shortages and personality clashes between those in command only served to worsen the existing problems. More than anything else, the main reason for the failure of the Dardanelles campaign was a lack of communication between the political decision makers and their military counterparts.

Churchill himself escaped fairly lightly from the more serious accusations which had been made against him. He was criticised for having advocated the initial attempt to force the Dardanelles by using ships alone, without due consideration of the opposing views offered by his naval advisers. But otherwise the Commission chose to blame the Dardanelles Committee leadership in a broad, collective way, meaning that Churchill was at least partially vindicated of blame. Yet the Dardanelles affair would still tarnish his reputation, and such close personal association with a military disaster continued to affect him until his response to the next major global conflict turned things in his favour. The whole affair was very illustrative of Churchill's character as somebody quick to present his own opinions on a subject, especially in regard to military strategy. Yet many would admit that Churchill's ability to cut through unnecessary bureaucracy was to be admired, and in the case of the Dardanelles, he certainly showed initiative in the absence of any creative solutions coming from the senior commanders and other politicians.

Asquith had resigned as Prime Minister in October 1916, to be succeeded by Churchill's long-term colleague David Lloyd George. Soldier Sam Davies, writing home to his sister from Macedonia on 8 December 1916, remarked on this change of government and suspected Churchill's influence to have played a part:

> What is really the trouble I wonder? What is Churchill after – fame or notoriety? One is as profitable as the other these days.

PREVIOUS PAGE Churchill, as Minister of Munitions, meets female workers at Georgetown's shell filling works near Glasgow during a visit on 9 October 1918. With his signature adorning every munition worker's identity pass, the workers would have felt an immediate connection to their 'boss'.

OPPOSITE This sketch by Henry Rushbury, commissioned by the Ministry of Information, presents a view of the crowded interior of Central Hall in Westminster on 4 July 1918. Churchill stands at a lectern to give a speech to a huge crowd of politicians and dignitaries in order to mark American Independence Day, telling them that 'Germany must be beaten, must know she is beaten, must feel she is beaten'.

THE FIRST WORLD WAR

Churchill watches the march past of the 47th Division as they formally enter the Grande Place in Lille, on 28 October 1918. In front of him is the Chief of Staff of the 47th Division, Lieutenant Colonel Bernard Montgomery, with whom he would work more closely during the next big conflict. Standing behind Churchill, wearing a bowler hat, is his private secretary Edward 'Eddie' Marsh.

Now that the Dardanelles Report had gone some way towards improving Churchill's reputation, Lloyd George decided to give him another opportunity in government by engaging him to investigate France's war effort in May 1917, in preparation for taking on the important role of Minister of Munitions in July. As somebody who was forever putting pressure on the government to influence war policy, it made sense for them to engage with Churchill as a full minister, rather than keeping him at arm's length where he might cause greater trouble. Yet the appointment proved controversial; both the Secretary of War and First Lord of the Admiralty threatened to resign if Churchill continued to involve himself in their respective areas of responsibility. But such differences had to be set aside for the Coalition government to continue.

The Ministry of Munitions was a relatively new government department, created in July 1915 to oversee the manufacture and provision of munitions for the war effort. Churchill would remain in this post for the remainder of the conflict, only giving it up in January 1919 when he moved to the War Office. Filled with enthusiasm over this new opportunity to influence policy, he embarked on an efficiency drive to streamline processes wherever possible. Bureaucracy in the Ministry was reduced, while the productivity of munitions workers was given priority at every opportunity. This meant that great effort was put into preventing and reducing strikes, a perhaps surprisingly common occurrence in Britain during the First World War. Churchill initially followed a benevolent approach by raising workers' wages, but when this failed to resolve disputes he eventually adopted a harsher attitude by threatening to conscript workers if they refused to comply.

Churchill remained unable to resist interfering in the affairs of his colleagues, using his munitions remit to involve himself in the government's wider war strategy at every opportunity. Reflecting his fascination with new technology, he constantly pushed for greater mechanisation in order to win the war and save lives – the use of aircraft, armoured vehicles and submarines should be increased, while artillery needed to be bigger and better. A regular visitor to the Western Front, this time as a civilian, he was keen to witness things for himself and to communicate directly with the armies in the field. This eagerness to gain a first-hand understanding of the situation endeared Churchill to the High Command, although his popularity among them would lead Lloyd George to accuse him of working for their military interests, rather than the Cabinet's political ones.

As the Minister of Munitions, Churchill's facsimile signature adorned every identification pass issued to munitions workers in the country's many factories; he visited numerous sites to inspect the work being done and boosted the morale of the mostly female workers. In support of her husband's role, Clementine organised special YMCA canteens to be made available in factories. It was perhaps this sense of responsibility for women munitions workers that influenced Churchill's support of the Representation of the People Act, which in February 1918 gave British women over the age of 30 the right to vote for the very first time. Yet he would remain somewhat cautious over the question of women's suffrage, actually deciding to oppose the extension of the franchise in subsequent years to younger women in case it might increase the Labour vote. Indeed, throughout the 1930s he would even suggest a link between extensions of the franchise in Europe and the rise of dictatorships. Perhaps his Victorian upbringing, combined with genuine concerns for the political status quo, caused him to doubt the wisdom of making significant changes to the voting system.

CHAPTER FOUR
BETWEEN THE WARS

The Armistice on 11 November 1918 brought an end to the fighting of the First World War, and would be followed almost immediately by a General Election in Britain on 14 December. Lloyd George's Coalition government of Liberals and Conservatives won a landslide victory, although the Conservatives held some two thirds of the overall coalition seats. Churchill remained the Liberal MP for Dundee and in January 1919 would take up a new role as Secretary of State for War and Air. One important responsibility that he now had to address would be the demobilisation of troops, many of whom had been fighting overseas for the previous few years. While many men would indeed return home to Britain, Churchill remained cautious of the need to retain a fighting force for deployment in a number of areas across the world, but in particular in occupied Germany as the Army of the Rhine; as a safeguard against expansion of the new Bolshevik Russia; and as a deterrent against potential revolution in Ireland.

Churchill's immediate fear was the situation in Russia. Bolshevism, which in 1917 had violently overthrown the Tsar in a communist revolution and taken over Russia as a 'dictatorship of the proletariat', was widely feared among the nations of Western Europe. Churchill, like many others in the British government, was totally opposed to Bolshevism, being concerned for the effect that social revolutionaries might have on the political stability of the country as well as the workforces of both Britain and its Empire. He therefore advocated sending some 59,000 British troops to bolster the White anti-Bolshevik forces who were still struggling to regain power in Russia, with these interventionist forces largely deployed in the areas around North Russia, the Baltic and the Caucasus.

However, it quickly became clear that the Whites and foreign interventionist forces were overwhelmed and unlikely to succeed, so an evacuation of British troops from the various fronts was eventually ordered towards the end of 1919. While the fighting had possibly assisted those nations in Central and Eastern Europe from withstanding a potential Bolshevik expansion into their territory, the Allied intervention also served to sow seeds of mistrust among the Russians, who would remain wary of the intentions of the Western powers for the foreseeable future. Churchill would claim many years later that if the interventionist forces had been better supported, they may have been able to destroy Bolshevism before it was given the chance to fully establish itself. Yet even in hindsight, this seems unlikely.

There was trouble too in Iraq, which had been occupied by the British immediately after the First World War until a League of Nations Mandate could put the nation more formally under their control. Rebellious tribes joined forces over the summer months of 1920 to seek independence from Britain's rule and establish an Arab government. Churchill's reaction was swift, installing pro-British rulers in Iraq and Transjordan while authorising two RAF squadrons to reinforce existing troops. Orders for the RAF to potentially bomb the Kurdish rebels from the air with poison gas were, in the event, never followed up. Considering the Mandate a drain on British resources, Churchill was

PREVIOUS PAGE British Ministers at the French Prime Minister Georges Clemenceau's house in Rue Nitot, Paris, following deliberations during the Paris Peace Conference in June 1919. Standing before the table in a lighter suit is British Prime Minister David Lloyd George, while Churchill can also be seen in the front row, fourth from right.

OPPOSITE As a member of the Army Council, Churchill visited the British Army of the Rhine occupying German territory in August 1919. His grey suit and top hat were a familiar sight to those receiving such inspections, which Churchill enjoyed as a means of involving himself in military matters.

Another image from Churchill's visit to the British Army of the Rhine in 1919. He is shown here alongside Field Marshal Sir William Robertson and other members of the Council while inspecting the Tank Corps, August 1919.

Courting the United States was not only an activity undertaken by Churchill during the Second World War. This photograph shows the Prince of Wales, the American General John Pershing, Churchill and the American Ambassador to Britain on their way to inspect American troops in Hyde Park, 19 July 1919.

actually more in favour of handing control of much of the territory back to Turkey at the earliest opportunity.

The other area of concern for Churchill was Ireland. Churchill's grandfather John Spencer-Churchill, the 7th Duke of Marlborough, had served as Viceroy of Ireland for a number of years from 1876 and the family name was therefore strongly linked with the pro-British political viewpoint of the Unionists. Indeed, Winston's ardent support of Ulster Unionism and his critical opinion on Irish independent self-government made him a controversial figure during his early political life. Yet by 1912 he had begun to soften his opposition by supporting the Home Rule Bill of that year, which would award dominion status to Ireland under overall British authority. Speaking in support of the creation of a Dublin Parliament, he was heckled and violently jostled by Unionists who remained in complete opposition to any such compromise to their cause. His heavy-handedness was also called into question when in March 1914 he deployed Royal Navy ships off the coast of Ulster in response to the threat of unrest generated by Sir Edward Carson's Ulster Volunteers, a paramilitary force founded to block Home Rule. Home Rule was signed into law in September 1914, but placed on hold as a result of the outbreak of the First World War. Feelings on the issues in Ireland continued to bristle, however, reaching their height at the republican rising in Dublin, which was put down in Easter 1916.

Sinn Fein's landslide victory in the December 1918 Irish elections led to them forming a breakaway government in January 1919 which declared independence for Ireland. This conflict gradually developed, fought between the Irish Republican Army (IRA) on one side and the Royal Irish Constabulary (RIC) on the other. The British government reinforced the RIC with paramilitary recruits from Britain, who began to be deployed in 1920 in their thousands. These were the infamous 'Black and Tans', made up largely from unemployed ex-soldiers, often ill-disciplined and traumatised by their war experiences. As the Secretary of State for War, Churchill was responsible for their recruitment and so quickly became seen as responsible for their brutal conduct, as they initiated reprisal attacks on civilian targets and behaved in a generally disorderly manner. Churchill chose not to speak out against their actions, possibly because his close friend, Lieutenant General Hugh Tudor, was overseeing the militarisation of these new constables. Criticism towards Churchill could neither be diverted by his half-hearted attempt to introduce greater authority through the creation of an Auxiliary Division of officers for the RIC, since these recruits suffered from much the same problems.

Churchill's involvement in Irish politics would continue when he changed roles in February 1921, becoming Secretary of State for the Colonies. He was then closely involved in the negotiations which would lead to the signing of the Anglo-Irish Treaty in December that year, effectively ending the Irish War of Independence. Despite their strongly opposing views, Churchill struck up a good relationship with one of the leading Republicans, Michael Collins. Responsibility for overseeing the transition of power to the new Irish government would also fall

OPPOSITE As Secretary of State for War and Air, Churchill arrives at a memorial service for airmen killed during the First World War being held at Westminster Abbey in London on 19 February 1919.

Equipment and supplies for White Russian forces being loaded off a ship at the Black Sea port of Novorossisk, 1920.

OPPOSITE Emir Abdullah I bin-Al Hussein greets Churchill as the British Colonial Secretary, alongside his wife Clementine, on their arrival for the Cairo Conference in March 1921. It was agreed at the conference that Emir Feisal should be offered the throne of Iraq, subject to approval by plebiscite. Emir Abdullah was offered the throne of Transjordan on similar terms.

PREVIOUS PAGE Troops of the Royal Irish Constabulary, supported by an armoured vehicle, lie along the edge of a road beside a field during an ambush in County Clare, Ireland, c.1920.

OPPOSITE Bust of Churchill by his cousin Clare Sheridan, December 1920.

to Churchill. Yet Republican disagreements over the Treaty, which declared the Irish Free State as a dominion of the United Kingdom, would lead to a near year-long civil war in Ireland between June 1922 and May 1923, between the Provisional government of Ireland on the one side and the anti-Treaty IRA on the other. Following the assassination of Field Marshal Sir Henry Wilson by the IRA in London in June 1922, Churchill called for the British Army to be drafted in to violently suppress the revolutionaries in Dublin. But fears that British involvement would only lead to further sectarian violence meant that the plan was dropped. The civil war was eventually won by the pro-Treaty National Army, yet the conflict left Irish society divided for many generations to come. Churchill's own relationship with Ireland was always determined by his loyalty to Britain and its Empire, yet his reputation for harshness in attempting to maintain British authority in Ireland means that he continues to be regarded with disdain by much of its population to this day.

Just as Churchill's role in Irish affairs would generate controversy, his statements on matters in Palestine would remain contentious. The Balfour Declaration of November 1917 had promised British support for a Jewish homeland based in Palestine, and at the end of the First World War a joint British, French and Arab administration occupied that region that had been previously controlled by Turkey. Following a League of Nations Mandate assigned in April 1920, Britain began to solely administer Palestine and, the following year, Transjordan. Churchill was an ardent Zionist who supported the notion of a Jewish homeland and, while visiting Palestine as Colonial Secretary, refused requests from Arab Palestinians to stop Jewish migration to the region. Only the riots which broke out in Jaffa during May 1921 encouraged him to introduce some temporary restrictions.

Churchill's period as Colonial Secretary also coincided with the so-called Chanak Crisis in September 1922, triggered by Turkish attempts to rid their territory of Greek occupiers while advancing against the British and French forces protecting the neutral Dardanelles strait. It seemed that a war between Turkey and Britain was about to erupt, yet few had the appetite for such a conflict so soon after the First World War. Despite Lloyd George and Churchill urging for action, the crisis was finally settled through negotiation. The greatest consequence was that Lloyd George's reputation suffered to the extent that Conservative MPs withdrew from the Coalition government and thereby triggered a General Election on 15 November 1922, which they easily won. Churchill lost his Dundee seat, which may in part have been due to his lack of campaigning while hospitalised with appendicitis. But it meant that now, for the first time in many years, Churchill was no longer a serving MP.

The following two years were an opportunity for Churchill to take stock of his life and re-assess his situation. The previous year he had suffered the double pain of losing both his mother, who passed away in June 1921, and his two-year-old daughter Marigold, who died of septicaemia in August. Further changes to his family occurred the

BETWEEN THE WARS

following year, with the birth of his fifth child, Mary, in September. The same month he purchased Chartwell house in Kent, which would serve as the main Churchill family home for the rest of his life; for the moment it would be occupied by Winston and Clementine, their four children, and a large domestic staff. Churchill would treat Chartwell with huge affection, considering it his special retreat away from the urgency and stresses of London and Westminster. When out of political office during the 1930s he would spend the majority of his time within its walls and grounds, regularly entertaining guests there by hosting lavish dinners and parties. For the immediate couple of years, however, he chose to holiday in the south of France where he concentrated on his writing. The first volume of his history of the First World War, *The World Crisis*, would appear in 1923.

Churchill's interest in politics was far from diminished, however. The General Election of December 1923 saw him stand again, this time as the Liberal candidate for Leicester West, but without success. Churchill's fears of socialism and in particular the threat posed by Soviet Russia were heightened by the policies of the new Labour government, led by Ramsay MacDonald. Disappointed by the Liberals' support of many Labour policies, Churchill therefore decided to stand as an independent candidate at the Westminster Abbey by-election on 19 March 1924, but was again defeated. It seemed that the Liberal Party were no longer strong enough to stop Labour without forming another coalition with the Conservatives, and so Churchill's strong dislike of socialism inspired him to enter into discussions with the Conservative leader Stanley Baldwin, who convinced him to stand at the next election on 29 October 1924. Winning the seat for Epping as a Constitutionalist (essentially an independent candidate standing against socialism), Churchill was asked by Baldwin to join the new Conservative government in the same role that Randolph Churchill had taken on some 38 years earlier. Winston became Chancellor of the Exchequer on 6 November, and in so doing formally returned to the Conservative Party, in which he would remain for the rest of his political career.

Churchill was rather an odd choice for Chancellor in many ways, as he could offer no prior experience of economics or the financial sector, and in fact had always suffered from his own poor management of his personal finances. Although he would remain in office until June 1929 and in that time deliver five budgets, he would be long associated with the poor decision in April 1925 to return Britain's economy back to the Gold Standard. Many economists, including those at the Bank of England, supported the strategy, for it was believed that tying the value of sterling to gold would boost the nation's prestige and prosperity. But others, including most notably the famous economist John Maynard Keynes, foresaw the potential problems which would manifest. An over-valuation of the British currency made the country's exports too expensive and raised interest rates, proving detrimental to businesses and leading directly to inflation and unemployment. In Churchill's defence, he went along with the Gold Standard strategy rather reluctantly, yet ultimately the blame was his to own and the economic

OPPOSITE The Spanish collier ship, the SS *Angel*, delivers coal to Britain during the 1926 General Strike, during which Churchill was serving as Chancellor of the Exchequer. The ship bears another link to Churchill, as it was formerly named the SS *River Clyde* when it was used to beach troops on the Gallipoli peninsula.

consequences were serious.

In many cases, business owners responded to the crisis by increasing working hours and lowering wages. The mining industry in particular was already suffering from serious competition in the face of cheaper imports from Germany, which had led British owners to lock out some 1.2 million workers in an attempt to resolve a pay dispute. Such a situation would create one of the most challenging moments for Churchill as Chancellor of the Exchequer, as the country was faced with a General Strike beginning on 6 May 1926, which would last for just over a week. Some 1.7 million workers, mainly from the transport and heavy industry sectors, refused to work in order to force the government to step in to protect workers' earnings. As these strikes were coordinated by the Trades Union Congress (TUC) and involved many of Britain's key public services and industries, the country was under threat of grinding to a halt.

Churchill's response to the threat of the General Strike was partly to follow his Liberal tendency towards social reform, sympathising with the miners and calling for the introduction of government subsidies to cover their wages. Yet he was also concerned by the wider threat that the Strike posed in encouraging socialist revolutionary activity and was keen above all to avoid anarchists bringing the country to a complete standstill. The government's immediate response was therefore to recruit volunteers, largely from the middle classes, in order to maintain essential services during the crisis. The printing industry was a particular concern, as striking workers might use their presses to publish socialist propaganda or indeed paralyse the nation's news coverage altogether. A government-run newspaper was therefore mooted, to deliver accurate reporting but above all to maintain calm during the crisis. As the Cabinet member with the most experience of journalism, Churchill was the obvious candidate to edit the *British Gazette*, as the official paper was named, although any impartiality was immediately forgotten.

Churchill embraced the opportunity with enthusiasm, requisitioning newsprint and improvising at every turn with a ramshackle staff. He personally wrote the paper's leading articles and ensured that his own viewpoint was presented as far as possible. Giving prominence to positive stories emphasising normality despite the strikes, while ignoring instances such as shortages of food or violence towards civil transport volunteers, the *British Gazette* proved immensely popular and achieved a circulation of well over two million readers. The General Strike would end on 12 May following surrender by the TUC in the face of the government's uncompromising attitude, leaving workers' conditions largely unchanged and unemployment rife.

Churchill's role as Chancellor would also involve him cutting expenditure on matters which would unwittingly cause him future problems. Although his campaign for the nation to invest heavily in re-armament in the decade leading up to the Second World War is widely known, the opposite was actually the case during his time as Chancellor. He strongly supported a policy of reducing expenditure on the armed forces, including even the Royal Navy, of which he had previously served as professional head. In keeping with the Conservative government's policies, he followed the belief that there was no risk of war for at least another decade and that the country could therefore afford to reduce its defence commitments. In an ironic turn of events, he would come to spend considerable energy over the following decade on arguing for the reversal of those very same policies that he had earlier supported.

The General Election of 30 May 1929 saw Churchill retain his Epping seat, yet the Conservatives overall were defeated. A new Labour government was formed under Ramsay MacDonald and Churchill therefore became a member of the Shadow Cabinet. The next year and a half were frustrating to Churchill, who disliked being in Opposition and increasingly found reasons to dislike his leader Stanley Baldwin's approach. Baldwin refused to accept Churchill's argument that a pact with the Liberals was necessary in order to beat Labour, while the issue of India proved to be particularly controversial. Baldwin supported the Labour government's proposal to grant dominion status to India, yet Churchill feared that this would simply lead to demands for full independence. As a Victorian brought up on the importance of the Empire and colonialism, the idea of losing the 'jewel in the crown' was too much for him to consider. Churchill decided to resign from the Shadow Cabinet in January 1931 over the issue, and so returned to the parliamentary back benches. The General Election of October that year saw him easily win his seat again at Epping, almost doubling his majority, yet the new Conservative government failed to offer him a ministerial position. Churchill's ongoing disagreements with Baldwin over Indian independence were undoubtedly taken as a leadership challenge and further such debate only led to Churchill being further sidelined. It seemed that his career as a political dynamo was over. Much of the rest of the 1930s would thus form what many would refer to as Churchill's 'wilderness years', when he remained out of the political spotlight.

CHAPTER FIVE
WILDERNESS YEARS

By the final months of 1931, it was obvious that Churchill was no longer a leading player in government. Although still serving as an MP, his influence on government policy was limited and any attempts to address major issues led to him being increasingly sidelined. He therefore began looking for a new purpose to keep himself busy. The secondary career that he consistently returned to throughout his life was his writing, and having suffered from significant financial losses as a result of the recent Wall Street Crash, books and articles for publication therefore remained a vital source for regular income.

Churchill's output as a writer was prodigious. By the end of his life, he had written some 6.1 million words, published in 37 books and over many hundreds of articles. He did make a brief attempt early on in his life to write fiction in the form of a single novel, *Savrola*, as well as a short story, but his literary output was overwhelmingly factual and largely based upon historical (or then contemporary) subjects with which he was connected. In this, he was emulating his father Randolph to a certain extent, who would write regularly on aspects of his political appointments and positions. It was Winston's own military experiences early on in his life which fed his journalism as a war correspondent, and this reportage would develop into a more literary career as he devoted time to biographies and longer works. It would be Churchill's histories of the two World Wars for which he would be best remembered. *The World Crisis* appeared as four volumes between 1923 and 1929, while his Second World War memoirs would eventually amount to an even greater work, running to six volumes published between 1948 and 1954.

While Churchill's books and articles would prove important to him, both as an intellectual stimulus to distract him from boredom as well as forming a reliable source of income, it was his public speaking engagements which tended to provide more lucrative opportunities. Lacking any immediately urgent parliamentary responsibilities, Churchill decided to return to the nation which he considered a second home, as he began another extensive lecture tour of North America. His last visit to the United States had coincided with the Wall Street Crash, when he had witnessed the huge scale of the financial disaster first-hand. His own investments had suffered dramatically, and the overall sense of desperation in New York in particular was highlighted by his witnessing the suicide of a banker jumping to his death from a skyscraper. This new visit would prove to be no less eventful.

Churchill, accompanied by Clementine and his daughter Diana, left for America on 5 December 1931. Not only had he agreed to a lucrative contract to deliver forty lectures at a guaranteed minimum fee of £10,000, but he had also wrangled an impressive deal with the *Daily Mail* newspaper to write a series of articles. By the standards of that era, his earnings from the trip were therefore expected to be huge. Churchill delivered his first lecture on 12 December at Worcester, Massachusetts to great success, but further plans would be put into turmoil by an unexpected accident.

The evening of 13 December saw Churchill invited to the home of

PREVIOUS PAGE Churchill's 'wilderness years' of the 1930s would allow him to indulge his hobby of painting throughout that decade, a pastime which helped him to avoid depression when his mind was not so active.

the financier and statesman Bernard Baruch in New York. Stepping out of a taxi and then preparing to cross Fifth Avenue at a corner, he forgot the American rules of the road and stepped without looking in front of a passing car. Churchill was hit and left in a crumpled heap by the roadside, still conscious but in great pain. He was rushed to Lenox Hill Hospital with a fractured nose and ribs, plus a deep cut to his forehead; pleurisy soon set in too, adding to his afflictions. Yet a week later he was considered well enough to return to his hotel, the Waldorf Astoria, for a fortnight of recuperation.

In a typically Churchillian manner, the patient would prove far from idle despite this setback to his lecture tour. He sought to benefit from the unfortunate accident by using it as the basis for one of his *Daily Mail* articles and, as his writings were also widely circulated across America itself, his celebrity status grew to the point where he would receive regular bundles of 'get well soon' cards and gifts from concerned supporters. Despite this being the era of Prohibition, Churchill managed to persuade his doctor to prescribe him regular doses of alcohol to aid his recovery. Following a brief holiday in the Bahamas, the tour resumed on 28 January 1932 and Churchill would travel almost every day for the next three weeks, delivering lectures in nineteen different American cities in an attempt to make up for the dates lost due to his accident.

Indeed, despite the initial setback, the trip would prove immensely successful. It had not only made Churchill a significant amount of money, but had also served to remind him of his popularity as a public speaker, at a time when his political reputation at home was at an all-time low. He had, perhaps most significantly, won over many Americans by talking of hope and confidence in the future, at a time when the nation was suffering so much from economic instability. The country would continue to associate this sense of optimism and stoicism with Churchill, which proved vital when he was working to forge closer ties between the United States and Britain in the following decade.

Another pastime which Churchill followed in order to keep himself busy during his 'wilderness years' was his hobby of painting. This was a diversion that he only began to consider in a serious way at the age of 40, in 1915, when he was feeling despondent at the criticism being directed towards him due to the Dardanelles debacle. His sister-in-law Lady Gwendoline Churchill was already an enthusiastic amateur painter, and suggested to Churchill that he take up the hobby in order to shift his mind off his troubles. Never one to take anything up in a half-hearted way, within days Churchill had purchased his own easel, oil paints, palette and brushes and was inviting professional painters to visit him in order that he might learn from them. Churchill would continue to paint whenever opportunity permitted throughout the rest of his life – even taking his painting equipment with him to the Western Front in 1916 – and developed into something of an expert. He only neglected his hobby during the Second World War, when more urgent priorities got in the way. Painting would also remain vital to Churchill

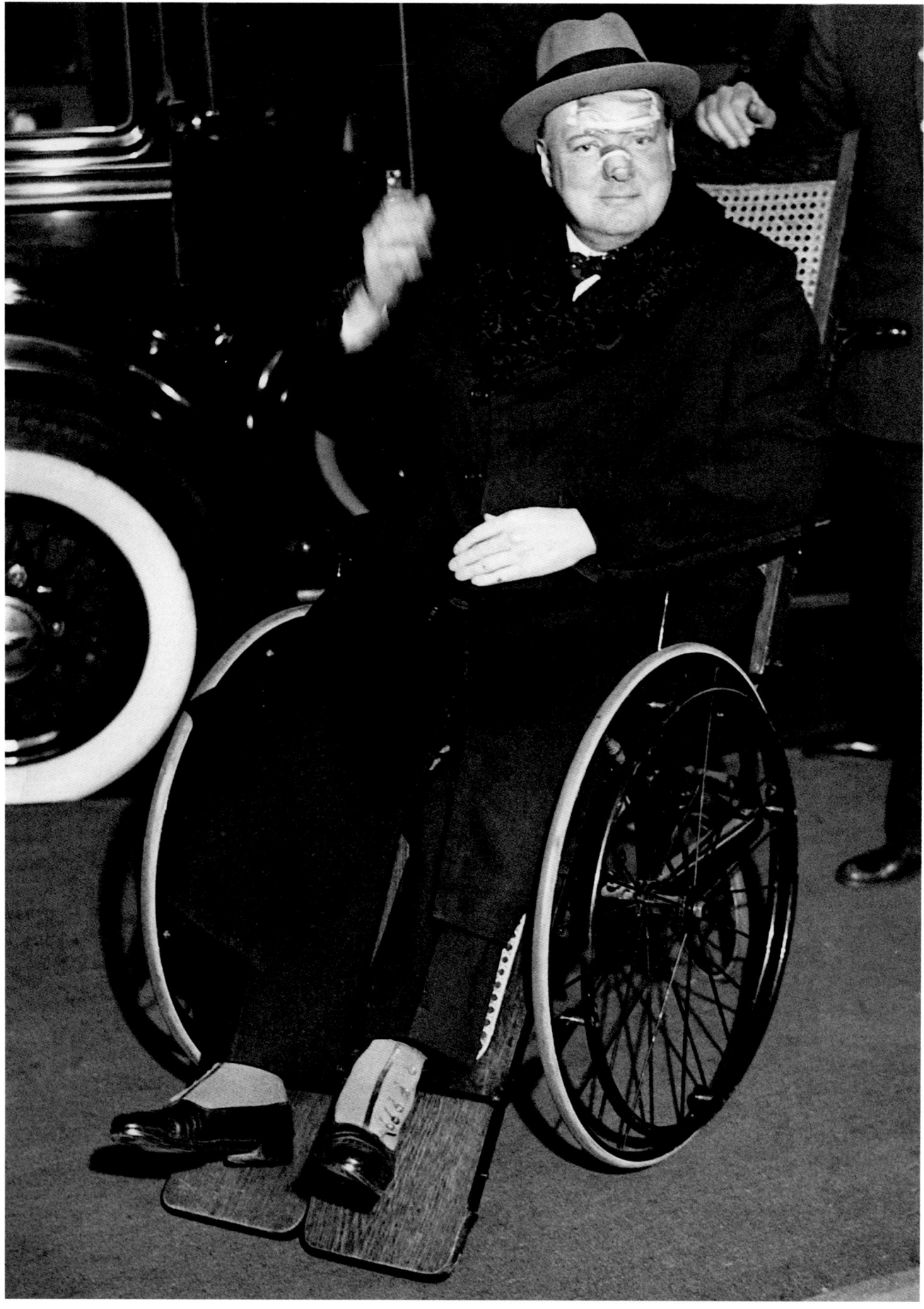

as a way to keep his mind active during those moments of gloominess which he increasingly associated with inactivity.

Never one to miss an opportunity to make money from writing, Churchill published articles on the pleasures to be gained from painting and in 1924, when the family moved into their new home of Chartwell, he was able to create a large artist's studio in the gardens, away from the main house, where he could paint without fear of interruption or distraction. This became one of his favourite refuges, especially during the 1930s, and throughout his life, Churchill studied the works of artists including Turner, Pissarro and Singer Sargent, and befriended others such as Walter Sickert. Many of these respected artists would visit Chartwell or accompany Churchill on painting trips. While some critics dismissed Churchill's skill as a painter, most could at least admire his use of bright colour in a style which perhaps shows more clearly than anything else his efforts to dispel the 'black dog' of depression.

A General Election of December 1935 saw the Conservatives return to power under Prime Minister Stanley Baldwin, but although Churchill once again comfortably won his Epping seat, he was not invited to take on ministerial office. Shortly afterwards, on 20 January 1936, King George V passed away. Churchill attended the lavish state funeral, mourning the wartime regent whom he had known so well, but welcomed the reign of the new King, Edward VIII. Clementine once described her husband as being one of the last true believers in the divine right of kings, and his support of Britain's royalty was unwavering.

Edward's rule was to be a short and controversial one, however. He had already embroiled himself in a number of affairs while Prince of Wales, but now he had become romantically linked with an American woman, Wallis Simpson, about to divorce her second husband. Edward soon declared their intention to marry. Baldwin and much of the government were firmly against the idea, fearing the constitutional repercussions. It was an era in which marriage to a twice-divorced woman was widely considered socially unacceptable, while the Church of England (of which Edward was the head) disapproved of marriage after divorce if a former spouse were still alive. With government resignations imminent, Edward had little option but to abdicate if he wanted to marry Mrs Simpson and avoid a constitutional crisis.

Churchill entangled himself in the matter by visiting Edward in an attempt to persuade him not to be too hasty in giving up the throne. He pleaded to Baldwin on the King's behalf for time to investigate a resolution to the problem, while being met with howls of derision in Parliament which cemented his split not only from the Conservative government, but seemingly also most public opinion. An emotional person and romantic at heart, Churchill misread the general mood of the country, which was against Churchill's dithering and rather preferred that the King should either abdicate or give up Mrs Simpson; in the event, he chose the former. On 11 December 1936 Edward VIII abdicated and was succeeded as King by his younger brother, who became George VI.

OPPOSITE Hit by a car during his visit to New York in December 1931, Churchill was forced to delay the rest of his lecture tour around North America. Here he can be seen leaving Lennox Hill Hospital on 31 December.

British press photographers take a break while waiting to photograph Wallace Simpson at the Villa Lou Viei, near Cannes, on 7 December 1936. Mrs Simpson had taken refuge at the home of her friends Herman and Katherine Rogers shortly after news of her relationship with King Edward VIII became public.

Due largely to his opposition to the Government of India Act, finally passed in 1935, Churchill's political isolation was almost complete. Yet the decade had seen the situation turn somewhat in his favour as the threat of war that he had been predicting for so long finally appeared to be emerging as a reality. Adolf Hitler became Chancellor of Germany on 30 January 1933, and Churchill was among the first to recognise the threat that this new regime posed. Germany's development of the Luftwaffe was a particular concern, since air power was predicted to be a deciding factor in any future conflict and, indeed, was shown to be the case in the Spanish Civil War beginning in July 1936. In that conflict, German and Italian aircraft contributed to the Nationalist cause by undertaking bombing raids which inflicted mass casualties and became infamous for their effect on civilian as well as military targets. Since the First World War, Britain had reduced spending on its own air force and navy and now Churchill led calls for the nation to reinstate funding and begin to rearm in order to defend itself in the face of a likely European war.

Speaking in the House of Commons, Churchill was vocal in denouncing Hitler's Nazi regime for its intolerance and aggression. Ellen Harris was a reporter for the Reuters News Agency and a regular visitor to the Commons, where she heard Churchill speak:

> I used to come home sometimes, literally and have a nightmare, before the war this was, when he used to talk and warn the government of what Germany was doing. How they were building up their forces, the ships they had… the planes they were building, and it was quite horrifying and I many a time had a nightmare over it. It turned out to be true, everything he said.

Churchill had in fact visited Germany in 1932 when he had narrowly avoided meeting Hitler himself. A mutual acquaintance tried to arrange a meeting, yet Hitler was allegedly offended by Churchill's criticism of his antisemitism and believed Churchill to be unimportant anyway, since he was out of political office at that time. But Churchill and other observers became increasingly aware throughout the second half of the 1930s of the worsening repression of Jews and other minority groups in Germany, as the wider introduction of racial laws made persecutions more obvious. Events such as the pogrom of 9–10 November 1938 (called '*Kristallnacht*' by its Nazi perpetrators), which resulted in hundreds of deaths and widespread damage to Jewish homes and businesses, served to highlight the aggression and militarisation which was now inherent within Germany. Yet Churchill's calls for greater British rearmament and government policies to encourage Jewish emigration to Palestine and elsewhere failed to elicit an effective response.

Baldwin resigned in May 1937 and the new Prime Minister Neville Chamberlain embraced a policy of appeasement. While the fascist regimes in both Germany and Italy challenged the balance of power in Europe by asserting themselves in ever greater ways, the

OPPOSITE Mussolini and Hitler pictured together during their first meeting in Venice, June 1934. The rise of fascist regimes in Europe was a serious concern to Churchill throughout the 1930s.

Neville Chamberlain meets with Hitler and other leaders to sign the Munich Agreement on 29 September 1938. Although intended to limit future German expansion in Europe, the Agreement was soon broken by Hitler, thus marking an end to Chamberlain's strategy of appeasement. From left to right: Chamberlain, French Prime Minister Edouard Daladier, Adolf Hitler, Italian leader Benito Mussolini and the Italian Foreign Minister Count Galeazzo Ciano.

WILDERNESS YEARS

British government sought to avoid war by offering them a string of political and material concessions. Churchill appealed personally to Chamberlain to reconsider the government's policy, but without success. He also called for a pact to be formed between European nations to defend each other against potential German aggression, but failed to achieve enough support for the idea for it to be properly pursued in time.

The *Anschluss* of 12 March 1938 saw the annexation of Austria to become part of Nazi Germany, and then the German occupation of the Sudetenland regions on 30 September laid the ground for a full invasion of Czechoslovakia on 15 March the following year. Numerous diplomatic agreements were broken, including most notably the Treaty of Versailles which had specifically been drawn up to curb German expansionism following the First World War. Yet the response of Britain and other European nations was extraordinarily restrained, as they preferred to fall back to diplomacy rather than stoke the fires of another major war. The annexation of Czechoslovakia in particular showed the ineffectiveness of British appeasement, since Hitler had broken the promises of peace he had made to Chamberlain just months before. Churchill and his increasing number of supporters called for the formation of a Coalition government to remove Chamberlain, and for the first time in many years, Churchill's name was being associated with a potential return to political power.

Appeasement had failed to curb German territorial expansion, and the next example would occur on 1 September 1939 with the invasion of Poland, barely a week after the signing of the Nazi-Soviet Pact which divided up large swathes of Polish territory between Germany and Soviet Russia. A major European war, involving Britain, was now inevitable.

OPPOSITE Churchill, having returned to office as the First Lord of the Admiralty, stands on the steps of the Admiralty building in Whitehall, London on 4 September 1939.

WILDERNESS YEARS

CHAPTER SIX

FIGHTING ALONE

Despite Churchill having spent much of the last decade in the political wilderness, he had devoted a considerable amount of time to pushing the British government to re-arm in the face of the increasingly militarised threat from Nazi Germany. Once Czechoslovakia was fully annexed by Hitler in March 1939, Churchill's opposition to the Chamberlain government's policy of appeasement became even more absolute, and both public opinion and the British newspapers began to show increasing support for Churchill to be admitted back into power. As he had been the most vocal person warning of a European war, it was only logical for him to now be given a role in trying to resolve it.

The Nazi invasion of Poland resulted in Britain declaring war against Germany on 3 September 1939, and on the very same day Churchill was reappointed as First Lord of the Admiralty, becoming a member of the government's War Cabinet. Churchill's appointment was a clear statement of purpose, giving official recognition not only to his strong opposition towards Nazism, but also restoring him to the role that he was perhaps best remembered for during the First World War. But the next few months would prove to be something of an anti-climax, as the war failed to develop in an obvious way; the emphasis in Britain was very much placed on preparation rather than actual fighting, and as such the period would become known as the 'Phoney War'.

That is not to say that there was no offensive action at all, since the beginning of the war at sea saw a number of significant moments in which Churchill, as First Lord of the Admiralty, was involved. Two key events in particular served to bolster Churchill's reputation. The Battle of the River Plate on 13 December 1939 was a successful response to the German raiders attacking merchant shipping in the South Atlantic and saw the German heavy cruiser *Admiral Graf Spee* scuttled in the neutral port of Montevideo. Then on 16 February the following year the German tanker *Altmark*, holding some 300 British naval prisoners of war, was boarded in neutral Norwegian waters and the prisoners were subsequently rescued. It would have seemed to many observers that Churchill's influence was already beginning to benefit the country.

By the end of April 1940 it was increasingly evident that Chamberlain was not the right person to lead Britain in a war. On 3 April he had scoffed at the notion that Hitler would embark on further territorial expansion, claiming that the Nazi leader had already 'missed the bus'. Yet only six days later, a major German invasion of neutral Denmark and Norway began, which fully cemented the failure of the British government's policy of appeasement. Attempts to stop the invasion by the Norwegian military aided by many thousand British, French and Polish troops proved unsuccessful, largely due to poor planning and organisation but also because military resources and supplies were inadequate at that time for such a major campaign. The Anglo-French expeditionary force therefore began to evacuate only weeks later.

It seemed that the situation with Norway and the wider question

PREVIOUS PAGE Churchill seated at his desk in the Map Room of the underground Cabinet War Rooms, May 1945.

OPPOSITE Now Prime Minister, Churchill leaves 10 Downing Street after attending a War Council meeting in May 1940.

FIGHTING ALONE

Professor Frederick Lindemann was a close friend and scientific adviser to Churchill. He is photographed here (left) alongside Admiral of the Fleet Sir Roger Keyes, at an artillery demonstration on 12 June 1941.

of Hitler's actions had come to a head, and widespread complaints about the way in which the government was handling the situation led to a major House of Commons debate, lasting for three days from 7 May. The opening day of the debate saw much vitriol and impassioned arguments. The only notable victories in the Norwegian campaign had been the naval Battles of Narvik, which had seen the German Navy defeated at sea, allowing liberation of the strategically important port of Narvik while pushing the Germans back towards the Swedish border. These successes were seen as being down to the leadership of Churchill and his Royal Navy, and Admiral of the Fleet Sir Roger Keyes (present during the debate as the MP for Portsmouth North) emphasised this point in the Commons to much applause. Churchill himself was put in an awkward position; while having already been vocal about the failings of appeasement, he was still a member of the Cabinet and as such was expected to speak on its behalf. This meant that he actually maintained considerable support on both sides of the debate.

But the most decisive part of the debate occurred towards the end of its first day, when MP Leo Amery (who had crossed to join the Liberal Party in December 1939 in opposition to Chamberlain's policies) made a passionate speech criticising the government's conduct, ending by quoting Oliver Cromwell but with direct reference to Neville Chamberlain:

> You have sat too long here for any good you have been doing. Depart, I say, and let us have done with you. In the name of God, go.

The following day saw the Labour Opposition call for a parliamentary division, which would require Members to vote on whether any confidence remained in the existing government. This the Chamberlain government narrowly won, yet with a drastically reduced majority. There was clearly little way that the present government could continue, and calls began to be heard for the creation of a national coalition to be formed under new leadership. Yet Labour refused to support a coalition under Chamberlain, meaning that a new Prime Minister needed to be found. Yvonne Green from Chelsea, whose wartime correspondence as a fire-watcher is now in the care of the Imperial War Museum archives, wrote home to her mother on 9 May 1940 and summed up the feelings of many people in Britain at that moment.

> Poor Mr Chamberlain is probably not feeling too bright after the division last night. I feel very sorry for him but maybe he is getting a little too old for good solid concentrated effort such as we need just now. I think Mr Churchill would be a good puller up of socks as P.M. Anyway I think it was pretty unfair of the Opposition to call for a division when they did – there doubtless needs some tightening up of Governmental activities but I don't think it was wise to do it, and show to the world in general what a rift in Parliament there was, at

the moment when we should all stick together as much as possible after the Norway fiasco. Everybody's <u>very</u> fed up about that. Poor Mr Chamberlain, he has tried so hard!

Many considered the natural choice for the new Prime Minister to be the Foreign Secretary, Lord Halifax. Yet Halifax himself refused the position, feeling that his existing presence in the House of Lords made him unsuitable. It was therefore Churchill who received the support of both Chamberlain and Halifax, as well as the Labour Party. In a moment of supreme irony, Churchill was therefore put into office with strong left-wing support, despite the fact that he had always declared himself a sworn enemy of socialism. Churchill accepted the role as Prime Minister of the new National government on 10 May 1940, and would remain as Premier until almost the very end of the conflict. However, his acceptance of the leadership would be a baptism by fire, since the early hours of 10 May were also marked by the proper end of the 'Phoney War', as German forces began an assault on the Low Countries and France.

One of Churchill's first acts as Prime Minister was to form a five-man War Cabinet, initially consisting of himself, Chamberlain, Halifax, and Labour's Clement Attlee and Arthur Greenwood. Additional members would join over the course of the war, perhaps most notably Ernest Bevin as Minister of Labour and National Service, but crucially Churchill himself took on the new role of Minister of Defence which ensured that he had personal control of the running of military policy throughout the war, albeit still subject to the support of the War Cabinet and the wider House of Commons.

Churchill was keen to surround himself with advisers whom he could rely on to provide the most accurate information and counsel, and among the most important of these was Professor Frederick Lindemann who, once Churchill became Prime Minister, was officially appointed as his chief scientific adviser. Lindemann had been one of Churchill's closest friends for many years, and despite a marked difference in the two men's outlook (Lindemann was a vegetarian teetotaller who did not smoke), they shared privileged backgrounds, an enthusiasm for scientific innovation and a common hatred for Nazism. Lindemann had already accompanied Churchill to the Admiralty in 1939 as an unpaid adviser. In the war years to come, Churchill would rely on 'The Prof's' ability to condense complicated scientific ideas into an understandable form. Lindemann's team distilled many varied sources of information into comprehensible statistics, to aid Churchill in his management of the different ministries while prioritising efficiency. Other scientists did sometimes question the data that Lindemann supplied, however, and although an ardent supporter for experimental weaponry he would often discourage Churchill from sharing Britain's own secrets with the United States.

It would take some time before Churchill was able to completely win over the different elements within the coalition and thereby unite the National government, as well as convince the wider population

Winston Churchill's Coalition Cabinet photographed in the garden of 10 Downing Street. Seen in the back row from left to right are: Sir Stafford Cripps (Ambassador to the Soviet Union), Ernest Bevin (Minister of Labour and National Service), Lord Beaverbrook (Minister of Aircraft Production) and Herbert Morrison (Minister of Supply). Those in the front row, from left to right are: Sir John Anderson (Home Secretary), Churchill, Clement Attlee (Lord Privy Seal) and Anthony Eden (Foreign Secretary). The image was most likely taken during the visit to London by Soviet Foreign Minister Vyacheslav Molotov in May 1942.

that he was the right man for the job. Perhaps surprisingly, there was still strong support for the idea of appeasement, with Halifax in particular suggesting that negotiation with Hitler was the best option by using Mussolini, leader of the still-neutral Italy, as an intermediary. Churchill's attitude however was to fight on, and with the support of both Attlee and Chamberlain as leaders of the two main political parties, Halifax and his supporters were left isolated. Appeasement and negotiation were seen as policies which would fail to work with an untrustworthy opponent such as Hitler, and such suggestions were from now on either marginalised or ignored, with continued belligerency the only honourable option to take.

Churchill's determination to fight was epitomised by the first speech he made as Prime Minister, to the Cabinet on 13 May 1940. It effectively served as a mission statement to which he would stay true throughout the conflict:

> I have nothing to offer but blood, toil, tears and sweat. We have before us an ordeal of the most grievous kind. You ask, what is our policy? I will say: it is to wage war by sea, land and air, with all our might and with all the strength that God can give us; to wage war against a monstrous tyranny, never surpassed in the dark, lamentable catalogue of human crime. That is our policy. You ask, what is our aim? I can answer in one word: it is victory, victory at all costs, victory in spite of all terror, victory, however long and hard the road may be; for without victory, there is no survival.

Churchill's public speeches would have a huge effect on the country's morale and willingness to fight, as journalist Ellen Harris recalled:

> By jingo, their effect on people! It was dynamite... Just the effect on myself, I could have picked up a gun and marched out to the front. He was terrific during the war, that man, he boosted the morale all the time.

But the first big test of Churchill's leadership was about to come. As German forces advanced through France and Belgium, they forced the Allies back towards the coast, from where a humiliating evacuation from Dunkirk and other French ports followed. By 4 June, almost 340,000 British and French troops had been rescued over a period of nine days and transported back to Britain. The consequences were clear: Britain was now isolated in Europe and in all likelihood facing an imminent German invasion. Churchill responded to such fears with another speech that afternoon which would again prove to both inspire and reassure. While recognising that 'wars are not won by evacuations' (and undoubtedly remembering his past involvement in the Gallipoli debacle of 1915), he went on to declare:

> We shall go on to the end. We shall fight in France, we shall fight on

Churchill at his seat in the Cabinet Room at No 10 Downing Street, London. This famous photographic portrait of the Prime Minister was taken by Cecil Beaton in September 1940.

Churchill helps to build a pillbox at Canford Cliffs, Poole, during a visit to Southern Command on 17 July 1940.

the seas and oceans, we shall fight with growing confidence and growing strength in the air. We shall defend our Island, whatever the cost may be. We shall fight on the beaches, we shall fight on the landing grounds, we shall fight in the fields and in the streets, we shall fight in the hills. We shall never surrender, and even if, which I do not for a moment believe, this Island or a large part of it were subjugated and starving, then our Empire beyond the seas, armed and guarded by the British Fleet, would carry on the struggle, until, in God's good time, the New World, with all its power and might, steps forth to the rescue and the liberation of the old.

Expectations within Britain of a German invasion were rife at the beginning of June 1940. Yet Hitler was reluctant to proceed immediately and still had hopes of forcing the country into submission through an extended aerial campaign. This was intended to crush the British resolve to fight on, while also serving to destroy the RAF air defences if an invasion was required after all. In a speech delivered to the House of Commons on 18 June, Churchill famously declared that:

> ...The Battle of France is over. I expect the Battle of Britain is about to begin. Hitler knows that he will have to break us in this island or lose the war. Let us therefore brace ourselves to our duty and so bear ourselves that if the British Commonwealth and Empire lasts for a thousand years, men will still say: 'This was their finest hour'.

The Battle of Britain would begin in July 1940 with regular German bombing raids on ports, airfields and industrial centres, initially mainly by day but from August also during the night. This summer of 1940 was the period when the war firmly made itself known in Britain, arriving on the very doorstep of ordinary people; responding to air raids and dealing with casualties and damage became an everyday occurrence, and the population looked to Churchill for leadership and support. It was no coincidence that his speeches and broadcasts during this early period of the war are among those which are now so celebrated, with his influential speech of 20 August, in which he memorably paid tribute to the fortitude of the Royal Air Force, coining one of Churchill's most famous turns of phrase.

> The gratitude of every home in our Island, in our Empire, and indeed throughout the world, except in the abodes of the guilty, goes out to the British airmen who, undaunted by odds, unwearied in their constant challenge and mortal danger, are turning the tide of the World War by their prowess and by their devotion. Never in the field of human conflict was so much owed by so many to so few.

The RAF doggedly stopped the Luftwaffe from gaining an advantage in the air battle and the deciding moment arrived on 15 September, later remembered as 'Battle of Britain Day', when the Luftwaffe launched their largest mass bombing attack yet, only to be decisively

In this unusual image, Churchill reads a newspaper while waiting at St Andrews railway station, Fife. This trip to Scotland involved him visiting Polish troops, inspecting coastal defences and touring the local Naval Establishment. Taken on 23 October 1940, the photograph shows a passing serviceman taking the opportunity to also snap the war leader.

OVERLEAF, LEFT This British propaganda poster links Churchill and his famous 'Let us go forward together' phrase with the Hurricane imagery of the Battle of Britain. The quotation is from his first speech as Prime Minister to the Commons, on 13 May 1940.

OVERLEAF, RIGHT Such was the success of the Churchill poster that a second version was prepared, aimed specifically at those from occupied Czechoslovakia. It reads: 'Czechs! The hour of your liberation has come!'

beaten by the RAF's defences. While bombing raids on Britain would continue, with the main target of German bombs switching to the civilian residents of British towns and cities, any hopes by Hitler of quickly beating Britain into submission were resolutely quashed. Britain had survived long enough to begin fighting back, and Churchill's reputation as a strong leader and figurehead for the country was now firmly established.

The air raids would continue for the foreseeable future, concentrating on London and the south-east of the country but also resulting in serious damage to many other cities and ports across the UK. As the end of the year approached, the raids became ever more intense and it was therefore all the more important that the Prime Minister should be seen to be maintaining a positive attitude to Britain surviving the experience. Churchill was adamant that he should play an important part in keeping the British people's spirits up, making sure that he was frequently seen in public and notably remaining in London despite the dangers from regular bombing. He also travelled widely across the country to visit factories, shipyards, bombed cities and military bases and appeared regularly in newsreels and press photographs, ensuring that his instantly recognisable image was seen and associated with progress. It was always part of Churchill's character to show little concern for his own safety, and when a bombing raid was expected, he would often go up onto the Whitehall roofs in order to watch it unfold.

But he was far from foolhardy, and realised that measures would need to be taken in order to protect himself and the leadership of the country from enemy bombing. It was for this purpose that construction of the underground Cabinet War Rooms (CWR) had already begun in 1938 during Chamberlain's premiership, to provide a safe facility beneath Whitehall for the government and military leadership to conduct war. At the height of the Blitz in October and November 1940 the majority of War Cabinet meetings took place there, and in December Churchill, Clementine and certain staff moved into an extension above the CWR which would become known as the No. 10 Annexe. Further construction added another thirty-four new underground rooms to house Joint Planning, Joint Intelligence and the London Controlling Section (who had responsibility for devising deception operations) as well as a telephone exchange, first aid room, canteen and suite for use by Churchill and his staff. Lieutenant Colonel Alec Bishop was part of the CWR staff and was therefore familiar with arrangements in the underground complex:

> Despite all the discomforts, life in 'The Annexe' was very stimulating and exciting. This was largely because of the presence and pervading influence of the Prime Minister. Mr Churchill started his day at seven a.m. when the telegrams which had come in overnight would be brought to him in bed, and he would dictate his observations and instructions on them. I remember on one occasion his shorthand typist coming out of his room in a state of considerable distress, and

when asked why she was upset, she explained that she had been unable to record accurately all that the Prime Minister had said, because he had omitted to put in his false teeth! However General Ismay, who the Prime Minister used to refer to as 'Sir Pug', came to the rescue on this occasion, as on many others.

Mr Churchill had a habit of climbing onto the roof of 'The Annexe' in the evenings wearing his blue siren suit and tin hat and watching the current air raid and the efforts of our searchlights to pick up the enemy bombers. He claimed that this interlude stimulated and helped him when he returned to work at his desk. It was not, however, quite so popular with his dinner guests, who he frequently invited to accompany him, and who could be seen following him with some reluctance up the stairs onto the roof. On another occasion he was standing at the entrance to the 'Annexe' watching an air raid when a splinter from a bomb which fell in St James's Park struck the wall

Churchill at work during a train journey through Kent, 20 June 1941. The Prime Minister spent a lot of time travelling around the country seeing things for himself, and often used such journeys to catch up on his correspondence.

Churchill inspects the ruins of Coventry Cathedral, 28 September 1941. By this time the city had suffered a number of bombing raids, the worst of which on the night of 14 November 1940 had resulted in the famous cathedral being set on fire by incendiaries.

Churchill observes a female riveter working on a Supermarine Spitfire, while visiting the Castle Bromwich factory in Birmingham on 28 September 1941. He was a regular visitor to such factories throughout the war.

Churchill would regularly tour the country's defences in order to boost morale, and any opportunity was taken for a memorable photograph to illustrate such duties. Here, Churchill is met by 'Billy' the goat, the mascot of the Royal Welch Fusiliers who were manning these particular defences in the south of England.

above our heads. The Prime Minister's personal bodyguard promptly threw his arms around him to protect him from injury. 'Unhand me, Sergeant Thompson', said Mr Churchill rather angrily. 'He is only doing his duty, Prime Minister', observed General Ismay. 'Does he think I have never been under fire before?' was the Prime Minister's retort.

London suffered its final heavy raid of the Blitz on 10 May 1941, with the CWR surviving intact. War Cabinet meetings could now resume at Downing Street or the House of Commons, and it was not until the appearance of the V2 threat in September 1944 that the CWR would host them again.

Churchill's personal morale during the Blitz had remained buoyant, and he consistently expressed confidence that Britain could resist the attacks. But he knew that in order to properly fight back, the combined efforts of Britain and the forces of its Empire and Commonwealth were almost certainly not enough. Victory over Nazi Germany could only happen once he had the full support of the United States, and this now became one of his main objectives.

Churchill had entered into a regular exchange of letters and telegrams with the US President Franklin D Roosevelt at the beginning of the war, playing up to his own American heritage and 'courting' Roosevelt, as he put it, to the benefit of Britain's interests. In response Roosevelt offered as much support as he reasonably could to Britain's war effort, despite the United States remaining neutral in the conflict in the face of nationwide disapproval of any American involvement in a European war. In September 1940 the two countries had signed an agreement in which fifty American destroyers were transferred to Britain in exchange for free US naval base rights in British territories. Then March 1941 saw the much more significant Lend-Lease Act, whereby the US gave Britain massive financial and material support as part of a policy of protecting its interests overseas. In the reassuring words of Harry Hopkins, the President's personal adviser who became vital to Churchill's long-standing efforts to bring the US into the war as Britain's ally, 'You are not fighting alone.'

Churchill and Roosevelt would finally meet properly in person on 9 August 1941, at a highly secret meeting on board the cruiser USS *Augusta* off the coast of Newfoundland. To begin with, Churchill unintentionally upset Roosevelt by saying how glad he was to meet him at last, forgetting that they had in fact met before, albeit briefly, in London in 1917. The two leaders did initially hold certain misgivings towards each other. To an American, Churchill epitomised the very worst of British aristocracy and imperialism, while he had also written critical appraisals of some of Roosevelt's politics. Yet they now enjoyed each other's company and forged a friendship which, while never forgetting their continued differences of opinion, served to forge a spirit of co-operation between the two nations.

During this first wartime meeting the two men agreed to a declaration that became known as the Atlantic Charter, in which both countries set out their mutual aims for the post-war world. These

Churchill insisted on a quiet working environment, and ordered his staff to use special typewriters that would reduce unnecessary noise. Remington 'noiseless' typewriters were soon imported from the United States and were in constant use in the Cabinet War Rooms, generating typed reports and memoranda that would have crossed the desks of Churchill and his War Cabinet.

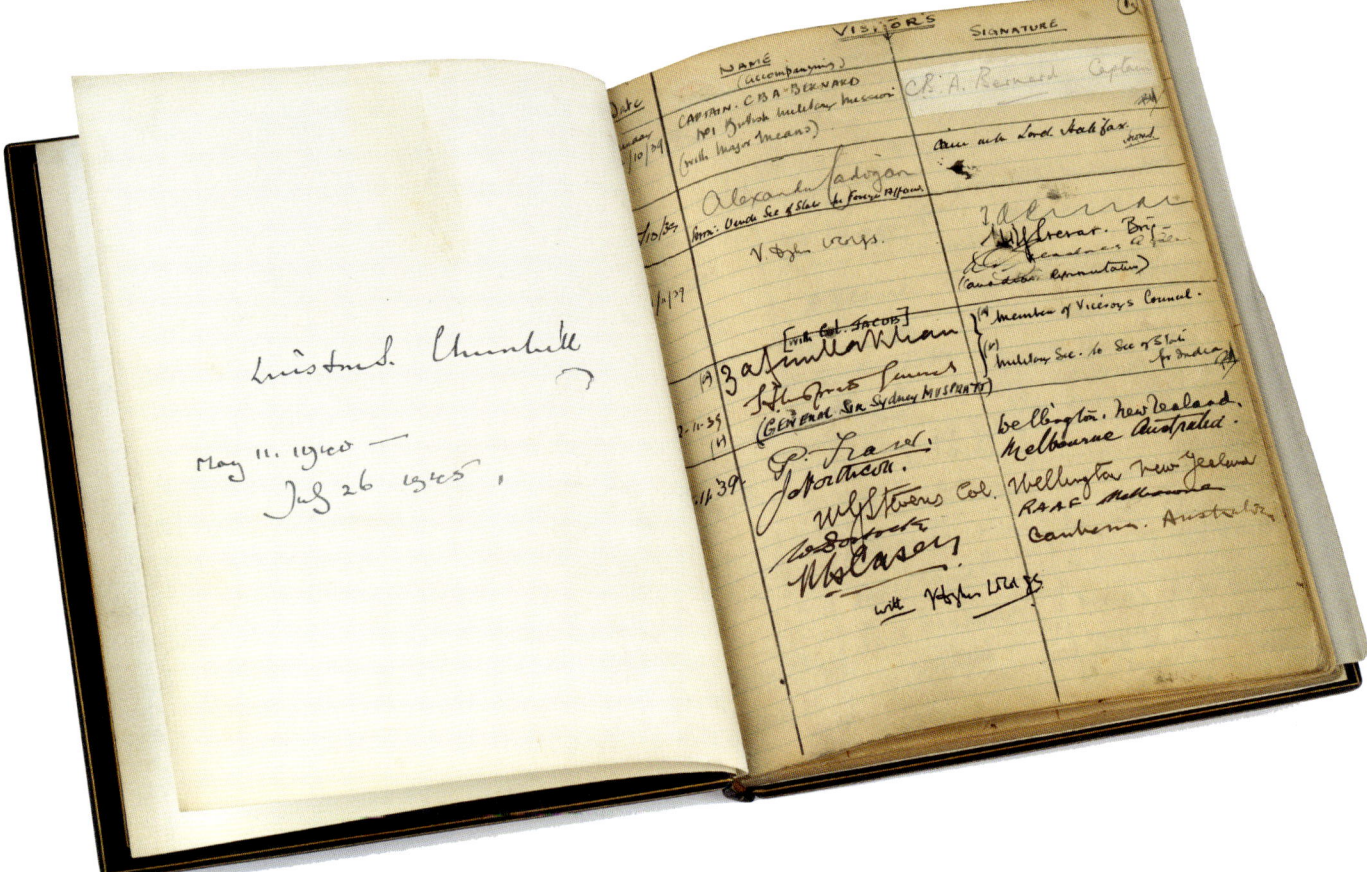

included, most notably, no territorial changes against the wishes of a country's population; restoration of self-government to those who wished it; freedom of world trade; abandonment of the use of force; and the establishment of peace, assuring all nations of their safety and 'freedom from fear and want'. The Charter was ratified by Britain's War Cabinet on 12 August, and allegiance to its principles was proclaimed by delegates of ten Allied nations almost six weeks later. By now, these Allies included the Soviet Union, following the Nazi invasion of its territory which began on 22 June 1941. The charter was subsequently endorsed by representatives from a total of 26 Allied nations meeting in Washington on 1 January 1942, in an event commonly acknowledged as the birth of what would become the United Nations.

The voyage back home across the Atlantic in the battleship HMS *Prince of Wales* was full of promise for Churchill and the ship's company, who fully realised the importance of their trip. Lieutenant Frank Goldsworthy RNVR later commented on the importance of their voyage:

> For me the most majestic moment of all that trip came when we swung away from our direct course to steam twice through the columns of a convoy of 72 ships headed for Britain with food and war

Visitors book compiled in the Cabinet War Rooms, containing the signatures of many VIPs who came to the site throughout the war. Churchill had his own page for his signature, with the dates indicating how he was present throughout much of the conflict.

OPPOSITE The Transatlantic Telephone Room in the underground Cabinet War Rooms, installed in 1943, provided Churchill with a means of talking securely with President Roosevelt.

FIGHTING ALONE

OPPOSITE The underground Cabinet War Rooms hosted crucial meetings when bombing made 10 Downing Street too dangerous to use. The tables in the War Cabinet meeting room shown here have been laid out to create a central well with enough space for three seats. It was here that the heads of the Army, Navy and Air Force would sit — eyeball to eyeball with the Prime Minister.

BELOW The wooden arms of Churchill's chair are gouged with scratch marks that indicate his nervous energy and the obvious tension of the hundreds of meetings that he presided over in this room. Deeper marks appear on the left arm of the chair, where Churchill's signet ring has made more prominent scratches.

FIGHTING ALONE

Churchill's bedroom in the Cabinet War Rooms includes a surprisingly small and basic bed, of the standard issue Civil Service type. He only slept here on three known occasions.

FIGHTING ALONE

Clementine Churchill would remain at her husband's side throughout his long eventful life. Here, the couple are shown on board a naval auxiliary patrol vessel as it travels down the Thames towards docks in east London on 25 September 1940.

Churchill and Clementine tour the smoking ruins of the Guildhall following the previous night of German bombing on the City of London, 30 December 1940. Such was the conflagration caused by the raid that the event became known as 'The Second Great Fire of London'.

supplies. I was standing a few feet from where Churchill was giving his well-known two-fingered V greeting in response to ship's sirens shrieking their acknowledgement to the flag hoist 'Good voyage – Churchill' flapping over our heads.

Throughout the second half of 1941, during this period when he was 'courting' the United States, Churchill had begun to adopt what would become one of his best-known mannerisms – the 'V for Victory' hand gesture. Although forever associated with Churchill, the symbol actually pre-dated him and began to see proper use from January 1941, when a radio broadcast by Victor de Laveleye, responsible for Belgian French-language broadcasts on the BBC, suggested that Belgians should use the letter ('V' for *Victoire*) as a rallying emblem during their country's occupation. Within weeks, the single letter was chalked on walls as graffiti throughout occupied towns, to indicate resistance to the Nazis.

Churchill and his daughter Mary, in Auxiliary Territorial Service (ATS) uniform, walk arm in arm aboard HMS *Duke of York* in mid-December 1941 just before the ship departed to take the Prime Minister across the Atlantic. There, he was to meet with Roosevelt for the Arcadia Conference in Washington DC.

Churchill addresses the Senate and House of Representatives of the US Congress, as well as members of the Cabinet and Supreme Court, in a worldwide broadcast at the Capitol in Washington DC on 26 December 1941. He was visiting for the war conference with Franklin D Roosevelt to discuss Allied strategy.

Inspired by this success, the BBC pushed for a wider 'V for Victory' campaign to promote the symbol, and in a speech on 19 July, Churchill himself approved the campaign and began to regularly use the hand gesture himself alongside, less commonly, the other Allied leaders. Normally the gesture would be made with the palm facing outwards, but often Churchill would make the gesture the other way round. By all accounts he expressed ignorance that this version was a common British insult, but even after being made aware, he refused to stop using the gesture that way – perhaps as a deliberate insult to his German enemy. The sign became a huge morale booster, as witnessed by soldier Ralph Thorogood, writing home to his family from Cape Town on 31 August 1942:

> You'll be interested to hear that I passed Winston Churchill in my truck when he was out here. He gave me the 'V' sign and I was extremely bucked. I could scarcely believe my eyes when I saw him.

Following months of fraught negotiation over the future of the Pacific region, Japan launched a major aerial attack on 7 December 1941 on the US naval base of Pearl Harbor in Hawaii, killing over 2,400 people and causing damage to twenty-one American ships. At the same time, separate attacks were carried out at other locations in the Pacific including against British territory in Malaya, Singapore and Hong Kong. Both the United States and Britain immediately declared war on Japan. Germany and Italy also declared war on the US in support of Japan, ensuring that America was now fully implicated in the global conflict. The Japanese attack on Malaya had resulted in the sinking of the battleships HMS *Repulse* and HMS *Prince of Wales* with the combined loss of over 800 British lives, the latter vessel having transported Churchill to Newfoundland only a few months before. Churchill would later describe this moment as causing the greatest shock he received during the entire war, yet the Japanese attacks also had a clear benefit to the British war effort by bringing America into the conflict and providing the support necessary to eventually bring a comprehensive victory.

OPPOSITE Churchill, cigar in mouth, gives his famous 'V' for victory sign during a visit to Bradford on 4 December 1942. Despite being informed that the palm-inwards version of the sign could be interpreted as a rude gesture, he continued to use this form on many occasions.

CHAPTER SEVEN
FIGHTING TOGETHER

Now that the United States was a formal war ally, Churchill was keen to meet again with Roosevelt. He did so in Washington DC for three weeks from 22 December 1941, taking in Christmas and New Year celebrations while discussing military strategy. Codenamed 'Arcadia', this conference was the first of many similar gatherings throughout the war between the Allied leaders, with the decisions made at such meetings remaining largely secret. In this case, the principle of 'Germany First' was agreed upon – the decision to prioritise beating Nazi Germany in Europe before victory over Japan in the Pacific. Both Churchill and Roosevelt agreed that Hitler was the main enemy, and the first Anglo-American attack was planned for North Africa: an invasion of French-controlled Algeria and Morocco, codenamed Operation 'Torch'.

On Boxing Day evening, after addressing the US Congress, Churchill suffered a minor heart attack. Refusing proper bed rest and seemingly shrugging off any health concerns, he instead proceeded by train to Ottawa, where he was to address the Canadian Parliament. Once again, Churchill managed to win over his audience and inspire many newspaper headlines around the world by making a jokey reference to how, at the beginning of the war, the French had predicted that Britain would fail to stand up to Hitler:

> When I warned them that Britain would fight on alone whatever they did, their generals told their Prime Minister and his divided Cabinet, 'In three weeks England will have her neck wrung like a chicken.' Some chicken! Some neck!

But despite this buoyant attitude, Churchill would return home to Britain at the end of January 1942 to face six months of repeated disaster. The Germans and Italians were achieving clear gains in North Africa and in the battle against Allied merchant shipping in the Atlantic, while the Japanese advances continued in Malaya and the Pacific. Realising that his leadership might be called into question, Churchill demanded a vote of confidence in Parliament – which he easily won. But the worst blow then occurred on 15 February, when Singapore fell to the Japanese. It was the largest British surrender in history, leading to well over 80,000 British and Commonwealth troops wounded or captured, and many thousands of civilians interned under harsh conditions for the rest of the war. It was a massive hit to British morale and a huge shock to Churchill personally. To add insult to injury, only a few days earlier the German battle cruisers *Scharnhorst* and *Gneisenau* had escaped from their port in Brest back to Germany via the English Channel, without hindrance from the Royal Navy.

By the end of April, the Japanese Army had successfully occupied most of Burma. The jungle terrain and extreme weather hampered any attempts to halt the invasion, while the occupation of the country meant that rice exports to other territories were suddenly curtailed. This had a massive impact on the Bengal and Bihar regions of British-ruled India, where the lack of rice combined with inflation, flooding

PREVIOUS PAGE Churchill fires a Thompson 'Tommy' submachine gun alongside Supreme Commander of the Allied Expeditionary Force General Dwight D Eisenhower, as American soldiers look on in southern England in late March 1944. Earlier images of Churchill with a Tommy gun had been used for enemy propaganda purposes, by depicting him as a gangster.

Despite suffering a heart attack mere days before, Churchill continued his North American visit by addressing the Canadian Parliament in Ottawa at the very end of December 1941.

Just as Churchill's image was used in Britain for morale-boosting potential, his caricature featured in enemy propaganda in a more critical way. This Belgian poster shows Churchill looking on as a woman and three children starve, with the text reading 'Monster, you make us suffer!'

Another wartime British propaganda poster featuring Churchill, this time making the comparison between the British leader and Hitler in order to encourage more economical cooking.

and crop disease led to a serious famine in which over 3 million people have been estimated to have died. The colonial authorities failed to realise the seriousness of the problem until it was too late, and Churchill's government came under fire for refusing to increase imports to India at a time when shipping was limited and in danger from Japanese submarines. But their decision was reversed once the full extent of the famine became known in September 1943, and more than double the usual imported grain and wheat was sent to India from alternative locations such as Australia. Lord Wavell was appointed as the new Viceroy of India and tasked with addressing the famine as a priority, yet further increased grain imports were consistently refused by Churchill, since shipping was being held in reserve for the following year's invasion of Normandy. The policies and actions of Churchill and the British government concerning the Bengal famine remain a subject of much debate and controversy.

Further disaster would occur in June 1942 as the Germans forged ahead in North Africa and pushed the Allies out of Libya, with the vital port of Tobruk captured on 21 June. The town had already been besieged for eight months during the previous year, before a relief force could arrive in December. Some 35,000 troops were captured, making the event second only to Singapore as the worst military blow inflicted on Britain so far. The Axis advance would only be halted by British successes in the First Battle of El Alamein during July, although the situation in North Africa remained precarious. Despite continuing fears over his health, Churchill insisted on visiting Cairo in August, on his way to Moscow, in order to inspect the troops and do his bit to raise morale as much as possible in the dire circumstances.

Throughout these moments of trouble, Churchill worked hard to maintain and strengthen the relationship between the Allied powers. He met with the Soviet Minister of Foreign Affairs, Vyacheslav Molotov, in London towards the end of May when they discussed the need for a Second Front to relieve pressure on the Soviet Union's ongoing battle against Nazi invasion. This was the message that Churchill took with him to Washington DC in June, when he met again with Roosevelt. But the liberation of Europe would have to wait, as the priority for discussion was Operation 'Torch', the long-planned Anglo-American landings in North Africa. In support of these, Churchill gratefully accepted an offer from the Americans of 300 Sherman tanks and 100 artillery guns to bolster the British Eighth Army.

On 12 August Churchill arrived in Moscow to meet with Stalin. Despite Churchill's fundamental hatred of communism (or 'Bolshevism' as he tended to refer to it), the two leaders worked hard to put aside their differences in order to work together as allies, being fully aware that they needed each other in order to beat Nazi Germany. Churchill was keen to support Stalin's war effort as much as he could, aware of the massive cost in human lives that this continued resistance was incurring for the Soviet Union. The huge extent of the Eastern Front also meant that Hitler was forced to commit vast amounts of troops and resource which might otherwise be utilised elsewhere. But

Churchill and the Soviet leader Joseph Stalin share a joke in the Kremlin, Moscow, in 1942. Churchill adopted a *Realpolitik* attitude towards Stalin, courting his support despite being aware of the atrocities he had sanctioned.

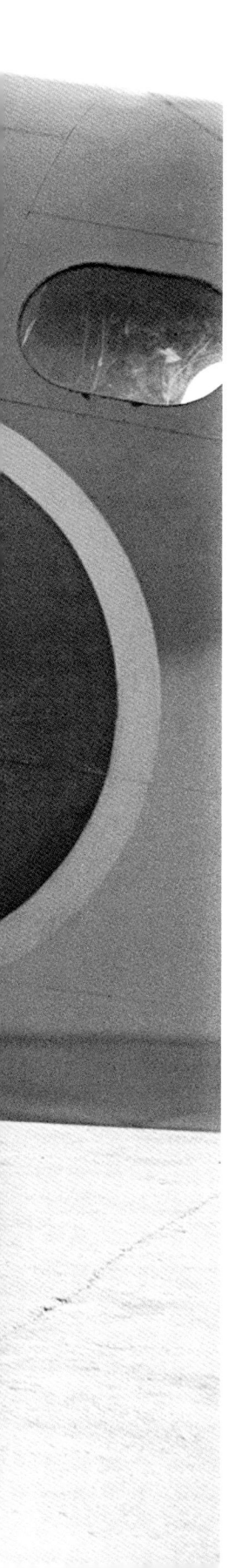

Churchill steps out of a Lockheed Lodestar aircraft after arriving in the Alamein area of the Western Desert, North Africa, on 7 August 1942. Following this visit, Churchill would appoint General Bernard Montgomery as the new commander of Eighth Army and the campaign would begin to swing in the Allies' favour for the first time.

Churchill was also conscious of the harsh manner in which Stalin had established power in Russia in the previous decade, by enforcing an economic strategy which had led to many deaths.

In turn, Stalin had an inherent mistrust of Churchill, whom he knew had always been critical of the Soviet Union. When told that the Second Front would have to wait until conditions were right, he responded with accusations of Britain's 'cowardice', resulting in Churchill threatening to go home and abandon the meeting. But after a subsequent private meeting in Stalin's apartment, involving copious amounts of food and drink, the two men finally bonded. Churchill left Moscow in a positive mood, proclaiming Stalin a 'great man' and promising that the Second Front would be launched as soon as was realistically possible. Despite his relations with the Soviet Union never being as close as those Churchill enjoyed with the United States, he continued to publicly praise Stalin for his strength, courage and good humour and would play up to the common Western portrayal of the Soviet leader as the benign 'Uncle Joe'.

It seemed to be the case that a change in military leadership would be required in order to improve the Allies' fortunes in North Africa, and in early August Churchill therefore appointed Field Marshal Alexander as the new Commander-in-Chief, Middle East. General William Gott was put in command of the Eighth Army, yet was killed before being able to take up the posting; he was therefore succeeded by General Bernard Montgomery. Churchill hoped that this new combination of leadership would turn the tide of the battle, and this indeed proved to be the case. The Second Battle of El Alamein came to an end on 11 November, and for the first time in the North African campaign, the Axis forces were sent into retreat. Later in the month, the German Sixth Army was successfully surrounded in the battle for Stalingrad, marking the first real indication that the Nazi attempt to occupy the city, and indeed their wider invasion of Soviet territory, would ultimately fail.

In jubilation at such positive news from North Africa, Churchill personally ordered that the church bells of Britain would be rung on the Sunday morning of 15 November for the first time in two and a half years. They had originally been silenced at the outbreak of war, and were only to be rung as a warning of imminent invasion. Also, on 10 November, Churchill used his annual Mansion House speech as Prime Minister to emphasise the acknowledged Allied victory at El Alamein:

> I have never promised anything but blood, tears, toil and sweat. Now, however, we have a new experience. We have victory. A remarkable and definite victory. A bright gleam has caught the helmets of our soldiers and warmed and cheered all our hearts... This battle was not fought for the sake of gaining positions or desert territory. General Alexander and General Montgomery fought it with one single idea – to destroy the armed force of the enemy, and to destroy it at the place where its disaster would be most far-reaching...
>
> This is not the end. It is not even the beginning of the end. But it

Churchill and General Sir Bernard Paget, Commander-in-Chief of Home Forces, watch infantry soldiers on a battle course at Barnard Castle infantry school, County Durham on 4 December 1942.

President Franklin D Roosevelt and Churchill make their statements to gathered Allied war correspondents at the Villa Dar es Saada during the Casablanca conference, 24 January 1943. The occasion appears very informal compared to similar summits held today.

is, perhaps, the end of the beginning.

As 1942 drew to a close, the future seemed to be getting brighter. Two days before Churchill's speech, the Anglo-American invasion of North Africa had begun, with the Italians and Germans being ultimately driven out of Libya and later suffering a final defeat in Tunisia. Victory in North Africa would prepare the way for an invasion of southern Europe the following year, before the large-scale Second Front in north-west Europe could begin.

For Churchill, the following year – 1943 – would be a year of travel. He would spend just over half the year away from Britain, travelling to meetings, attending conferences or recuperating from a number of health scares. He met Roosevelt again in Casablanca in January, this time alongside Charles de Gaulle, representing the Free French. An agreement was reached that they would accept nothing less than an unconditional surrender by Germany. By the time that Churchill returned to Britain on 7 February, he had been travelling for over a month, and it is perhaps not surprising that such exertions took their toll once again on his health. Five days after his return he contracted pneumonia and moved to the Prime Minister's country estate of Chequers for a month's rest and recuperation. But his eagerness for travel could not be stopped, and he crossed the Atlantic twice that year to meet with his North American allies, firstly visiting Washington DC in May and then Quebec in August. He made the trip to Cairo again in November, this time meeting Roosevelt alongside the Chinese leader Chiang Kai-shek.

The summer months also saw the first Allied landings in occupied Europe. Both Churchill and the Americans were nervous about committing too soon to a campaign in north-west Europe, fearing a stalemate situation like the Western Front of the First World War and realising that significant planning and resource needed to be put into the idea. Churchill instead suggested that what he called 'the soft belly of the Mediterranean' should be the initial target instead. The capture of Sicily would be the first step, beginning with Allied landings there on 19 July. The success of the operation would lead directly to the collapse of the fascist regime in Italy and the overthrow of Mussolini, who was arrested by order of King Victor Emmanuel III on 25 July. Once Sicily was fully captured by mid-August, the invasion of mainland Italy would follow.

The British Eighth Army and US Fifth Army landed in southern Italy on 3 September, and within five days Italy called an armistice. Yet the fighting did not stop, as German troops took control of much of the northern and central parts of the country alongside the remaining fascist forces, and fought to stop the Allied advance northwards. The mountainous terrain of the Apennines proved particularly difficult for the Allies to cross, and a series of offensives throughout the early months of 1944 would be necessary before Rome was finally liberated on 4 June. The Italian campaign would be a difficult and bloody one, and while few questioned Churchill's wisdom in recommending Italy over Normandy, progress was much more difficult to achieve than had first been expected.

The most important conference of 1943 was undoubtedly that held

Churchill talks to his son, Captain Randolph Churchill, at a North African airfield following the end of the Desert War in February 1943. As they stand under the wing of an aircraft, a cameraman can be seen behind them filming the encounter for a newsreel. Originally commissioned into the 4th Queen's Own Hussars, his father's old regiment, Randolph had by this time transferred to the Intelligence Staff at Middle East HQ.

Churchill addresses the ship's company of the battlecruiser HMS *Renown* before disembarking at Greenock in Scotland on 20 September 1943. The ship had brought him home from Canada, where he had met with President Roosevelt to discuss plans for the D-Day invasion, and the same vessel would convey him to the Cairo Conference a few weeks later.

FIGHTING TOGETHER

Marshal Kliment Voroshilov shows the Sword of Stalingrad to President Franklin D Roosevelt in the conference room at the Soviet Legation in Tehran, Iran, on 28 November 1943. Churchill and Stalin look on. The sword had been presented to Stalin by Churchill as a tribute to the Soviet defenders of the Russian city.

Churchill with President Roosevelt and Marshal Stalin at a dinner party held at the British Legation during the Tehran conference. The conference happened to coincide with Churchill's 69th birthday on 30 November 1943, and the Allied leaders were invited to celebrate with him.

Churchill sits in the sunshine in Marrakesh, Morocco, in December 1943 while convalescencing. He had fallen ill with pneumonia, and sought to recover in one of his favourite holiday destinations. He would return regularly to Marrakesh throughout his life.

OPPOSITE This poster was printed in 1943 for the passengers and staff of London Transport as a morale-boosting exercise in recalling important occasions that illustrated the nation's heritage. Here, Churchill's famous speech of three years previously is recalled, in which he promised that Britain would 'never surrender'. Already, Churchill was being associated with the rich history of the country; other posters in the same series included William Pitt and Horatio Nelson.

in Tehran, from 28 November. This meeting in the Iranian capital would last for four days and prove an important opportunity for two reasons: crucial progress would be made in terms of the Allied war strategy, but it would also be the first occasion when all of the 'Big Three' leaders – Churchill, Roosevelt and Stalin – would meet in person. All three agreed to commit to establishing the long called-for Second Front at the earliest opportunity, and decided that this would involve a cross-Channel invasion of north-west Europe, to be conducted in May the following year. They also debated operations against Japan as well as aspects of the post-war fate of Europe, such as the question of Poland's borders.

Roosevelt laboured hard to court Stalin's support at Tehran, which annoyed Churchill who felt increasingly side-lined. Yet Britain lacked the vast resources of both the United States and Soviet Union, and was therefore always going to be the junior partner in such an alliance. Churchill took the opportunity to seize the high ground, by presenting a gift from the King to Stalin – the 'Sword of Stalingrad' – in order to honour the successful Russian resistance to the German attempt to occupy their city. The gift brought tears to Stalin's eyes and Churchill received a great bear hug in return. Yet relations at the conference were far from smooth, and one tense moment saw Churchill march out of the room in disgust when Stalin suggested executing many thousands of German officers in order to prevent another war. While Roosevelt jokingly suggested that only 49,000 deaths might be enough, Stalin had to encourage Churchill back into the room by explaining that he had made a joke in poor taste. But the British leader was fully aware of the atrocities which Stalin had already supported and had to carefully compose himself before continuing the discussions.

Travelling on with Roosevelt to Cairo and then Tunis, Churchill again suffered serious heart problems and was forced to remain in Tunis for rest and recuperation until almost the end of the year. Clementine flew out to keep him company, and together they then spent time in Marrakesh before returning to London on the morning of 18 January 1944. In a decision typical of Churchill's stoicism, despite the strains of constant travel and his clear health problems, he chose to address the House of Commons that same afternoon.

According to the original wartime caption for this undated photograph, the sergeant pictured travelled from Canada to join the RAF and on arrival in England purchased a bulldog. He christened this mascot 'Churchill'.

FIGHTING TOGETHER

A rare wartime colour photograph showing Churchill, in the uniform of an air commodore, alongside General Charles de Gaulle, leader of the Free French. The occasion was an inspection of French troops at Marrakesh in January 1944. Both leaders actively disliked each other, yet hid their mutual animosity for the camera.

CHAPTER EIGHT
THE PATH TO VICTORY

Despite the Allied campaign in Italy becoming bogged down, Churchill threw his enthusiasm behind the long-planned Operation 'Overlord': the landing of Allied troops in north-west Europe. In many ways the opening of this Second Front would be a culmination of Churchill's long-term effort to foster relations between Britain and the United States. But the course of planning had been far from smooth. Stalin in particular had been pushing for a Second Front to be launched much sooner, in order to relieve pressure on his own army fighting to repulse the Nazi invasion of Soviet Russia. Yet Churchill and his Chiefs of Staff preferred to be more cautious, feeling that further preparation and stockpiling of troops and materiel in readiness was necessary. The operation would have to be massive and huge casualty statistics were predicted as inevitable but necessary in order to gain a foothold on the continent.

An elaborate D-Day deception plan, Operation 'Fortitude', was designed to divert attention away from the landing sites in Normandy. This received the enthusiastic support of Churchill, as elaborate efforts were made to convince the Germans that Norway or the Pas de Calais region of France would be the intended invasion targets. Churchill's long-standing fascination with new technology and innovation also fed into the D-Day operation, as he stood firmly behind multiple new developments to aid the amphibious landing. The design and production of new vehicles and equipment would be needed, as well as the adaptation of existing ones to allow them to take the beaches quickly and efficiently. One particularly important innovation were the Mulberry harbours, temporary artificial harbours which were floated into position to meet the need for port facilities before existing French ports could be liberated and restored. Churchill pushed for such new ideas regularly, and gave full encouragement and support for them whenever he could.

Churchill, as always, was keen to be at the centre of any action, either to see for himself what the true situation may be, or to play a direct part in influencing its outcome. He had been criticised in the past on many occasions for what some considered this 'grandstanding', yet his natural inquisitiveness tended to be a stronger factor than any desire for self-publicity. Considering the effort he had put into attaining American involvement in the war and all the resources that brought with it, it is perhaps not surprising that as D-Day approached he expressed a desire to be there in person as the operation was launched. His intention was to be on board the cruiser HMS *Belfast* on D-Day, viewing the landings from as near as possible to the Normandy beaches. Realising that he would receive widespread resistance to this idea, Churchill even threatened to commission himself into the Royal Navy in order to justify his presence.

The British Chiefs of Staff and General Eisenhower, the Supreme Allied Commander, were faced with an awkward situation. Their solution to keep the Prime Minister out of trouble was to appeal to perhaps the only person he would listen to – the King. George VI therefore wrote to Churchill on 2 June, mere days before the operation,

PREVIOUS PAGE Lieutenant General Sir Miles Dempsey, commanding the British Second Army, points out a section of the front to Churchill during a visit to Caen in Normandy on 22 July 1944. Also pictured are Lieutenant General Guy Simonds (left), commanding II Canadian Corps, and the 21st Army Group commander General Bernard Montgomery (right).

OPPOSITE Churchill rests while enjoying the summer sun aboard a destroyer taking him on a tour of the Normandy invasion beaches, 12 June 1944, some six days after the Allied landings

Churchill observes the destruction at Caen in France, with Montgomery (second from right) and Lieutenant General Sir Miles Dempsey (centre) on 22 July 1944. The city was devastated by Allied bombing over many weeks before it could be liberated.

Churchill and General Montgomery meet in Normandy in front of Montgomery's caravan, located at his headquarters at Chateau Creully, on 7 August 1944. Monty introduces his puppy, named 'Rommel', in tribute to his Desert War foe.

in order to ask him to reconsider:

> My Dear Winston, I want to make one more appeal to you not to go to sea on D day. Please consider my own position. I am a younger man than you, I am a sailor, and as king I am the head of all three services. There is nothing I would like better than to go to sea but I have agreed to stay at home; is it fair that you should then do exactly what I should have liked to do myself?
>
> … Then there is your own position. You will see very little, you will seem a considerable risk, you will be inaccessible at a critical time when vital decisions might have to be taken, and however unobtrusive you may be, your very presence on board is bound to be a very heavy additional responsibility to the Admiral and Captain.
>
> … I ask you most earnestly to consider the whole question again, and not let your personal wishes which I very well understand lead you to depart from your own high standard of duty to the State.

The royal pressure finally led Churchill to concede that his duty was to remain at home. But he could not resist travelling to Normandy at the first opportunity and on 12 June, only some six days after the invasion began, he landed on the continent to view the beachheads for himself and inspect progress. This first visit lasted only a day and gave him a brief opportunity to meet with General Montgomery, in command of the ground forces now launching the campaign to liberate Normandy, but he would return towards the end of the following month to Cherbourg and Arromanches, to check on progress. On this latter occasion Lieutenant Commander E B Rhead was serving as an officer in the battle cruiser HMS *Enterprise*:

> Our instructions were to proceed to Arromanches and act as floating hotel for the Prime Minister – Winston Churchill. Frantic preparations – Captain moved out of his quarters to his sea cabin on the bridge, cabins for staff had to be arranged and not least we had to get to Arromanches. By this time it was well organised with a Harbour Master and some anti-aircraft defences. We duly arrived and moored stern on to the concrete breakwaters… The great man duly arrived late afternoon, again with Peter Scott in his Motor Torpedo Boat (MTB) and fortunately only two staff – a secretary – male and Commander Thompson RN who was his naval ADC and the one man who had most influence with Churchill. We made him an honorary member of the wardroom mess, knowing his strict adherence to naval etiquette he was certain to come to dinner.
>
> The first night was uneventful and he stayed and dined in his cabin. There was an air raid that night and we were at action stations. There was a plaintive cry over the telephone from a sub-lieutenant on duty on the quarter deck saying Churchill was on deck without a tin hat and would not go below BUT just commandeered sub-lieutenant's tin hat and announced he was staying to see the fun. Commander Thompson eventually persuaded him to go below, but

OPPOSITE A memorandum from Churchill issued on 30 May 1942, calling for further investigation into what would become 'Mulberry Harbours', the artificial harbours necessary to support the amphibious landings on D-Day. Churchill was fascinated by new technology and inventions, and could not resist involving himself in such things wherever possible.

10, Downing Street,
Whitehall.

PIERS FOR USE ON BEACHES

C.C.O. or deputy.

They must float up and down with the tide. The anchor problem must be mastered. Let me have the best solution worked out. Don't argue the matter. The difficulties will argue for themselves.

30. 5. 42.

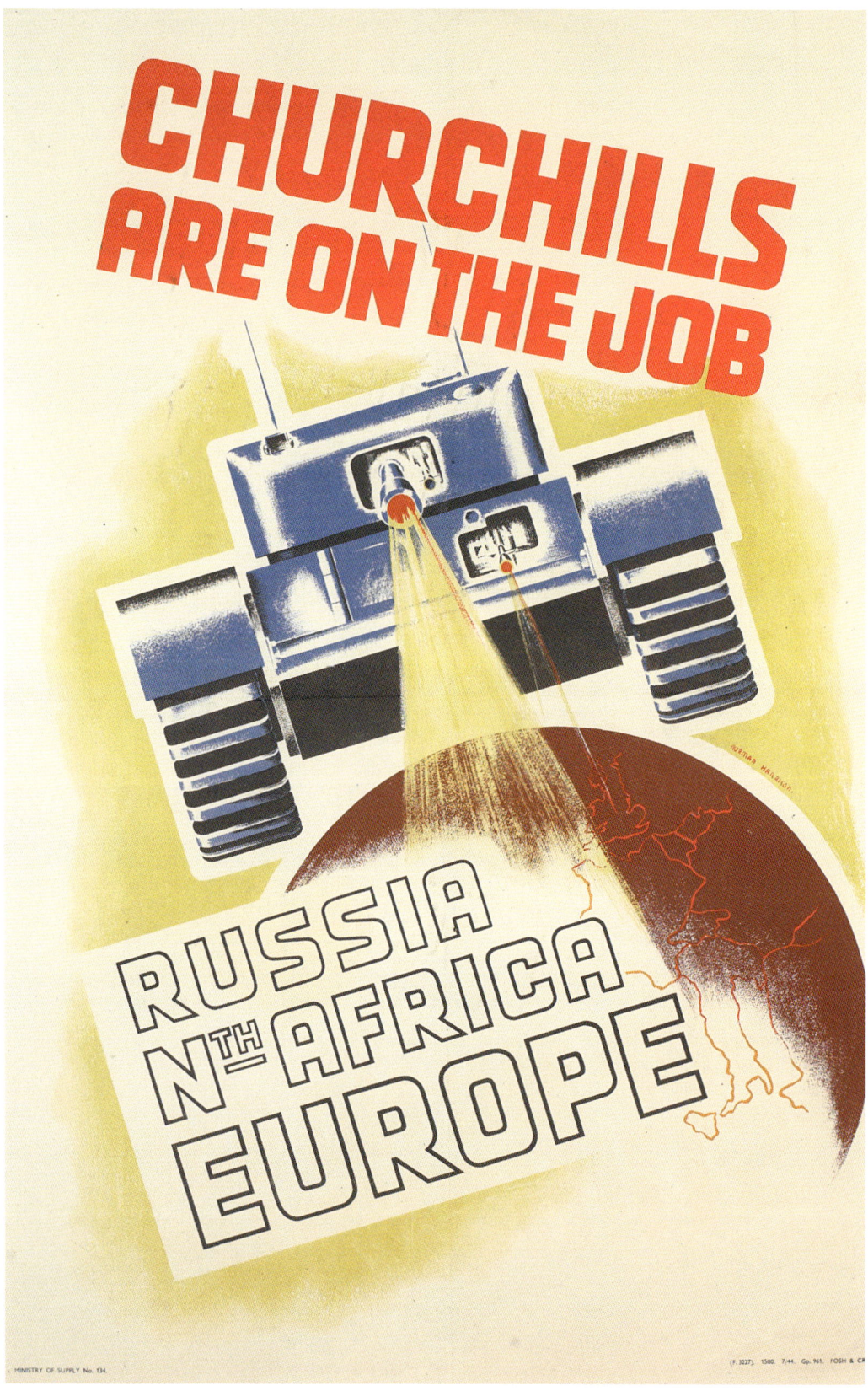

This poster, issued in July 1944, exhorts the importance of Churchill tanks to the various campaigns being fought across the world. The immediately recognisable name on the poster also serves to promote the importance of the current British leader, associating him with stoicism and strength.

the raid ended anyway.

He went ashore the next day and returned in the late afternoon again in Peter Scott's MTB. Our Captain sent a young sub-lieutenant to the bottom of the gangway to give Churchill a hand jumping from the MTB to gangway. The young man trying to be helpful put out a hand and got a blast of language – 'to get out of my way'. Churchill announced he would join us for dinner in the Wardroom that evening and duly arrived. After dinner he made a major political speech on the overall situation as he saw it. Not only on Europe but the world and said things he probably would not have said with press present... we understood him to hint that things political in Germany were probably going our way. Afterwards he suggested we sang 'Rule Britannia'. The padre could play the piano and bashed away and we all sang the first verse very lustily, and struggled through the second verse... He sang the last verse all alone beating time with his cigar.

With the Second Front now firmly established, important planning work was still to be done in order to prepare for the end of the war. Churchill spent much of the second half of 1944 attending various conferences at which the Allied leaders discussed the administration of occupied territory and how Europe might look once Nazi Germany had been beaten. He met first with Roosevelt in Quebec between 12 and 16 September, where the demilitarisation of Germany was discussed. Then the following month, Churchill flew to Moscow to meet again with Stalin where the post-war fate of the Balkan nations was the prime topic for discussion.

Most controversially, at Moscow, Churchill and Stalin came to a secret informal agreement over how control of disputed territory in Eastern Europe was to be split between the Soviet Union and the democratic Western nations. Roosevelt had been tentatively consulted beforehand, yet the United States were largely kept out of the discussions which led to a 'percentages agreement' in which Britain would largely control Greece, while other territories such as Romania and Bulgaria would be primarily Russian. British control over Greece was considered of vital importance to Churchill, who feared that Soviet support of the Greek National Liberation Front (EAM) and its military arm (ELAS) would ensure that Greece became communist and thereby threaten the eastern Mediterranean. To prevent this happening, he was content to give over the rest of the Balkans to communism.

With the Red Army invading Romania in August 1944, the German and Bulgarian troops occupying neighbouring Greece withdrew by October; the capture of the Romanian oil fields and strong Greek resistance meant that continued occupation had little purpose. British troops arrived in Athens on 14 October, with the Greek government returning from exile to re-establish itself. But conflict soon erupted between the monarchist Right and the communist/republican Left, with violent demonstrations by ELAS on 3 December which led to the establishment of martial law by the British.

This internal conflict in Greece between the British occupying

Churchill discusses the battle situation in Italy with the Commander of the Eighth Army, Lieutenant General Sir Oliver Leese (left) and the Supreme Allied Commander of the Mediterranean, General Sir Harold Alexander, at Leese's headquarters in the Monte Maggio area of Italy, 26 August 1944.

While inspecting reconstruction work in Cherbourg, Churchill has his cigar lit by a French worker, much to the amusement of the surrounding crowd and Churchill's fellow passenger, Major General Cecil Moore. General Moore was the US Army's Chief Engineer of the European Theatre of Operations, c. late July 1944.

Churchill visits a forward observation post near Florence in Italy, to watch an artillery bombardment in action on 20 August 1944. The original wartime caption states: 'As the shoot progressed, he removed his jacket, lit a cigar and settled down to watch the fun. As the artillery plastered the target area, he mopped his brow in sympathy with the hot time the enemy was experiencing'.

OPPOSITE Churchill and General Charles de Gaulle, leader of the Free French forces, at the French Armistice Day parade in Paris on 11 November 1944. The French capital had finally been liberated from several years of German occupation just over two months earlier, at the very end of August.

troops and the Greek force who had previously fought alongside them against the Nazis, proved to be an embarrassing situation which needed to be quickly resolved. Churchill rushed to Athens that Christmas, accompanied by General Alexander and senior Cabinet members, to hold a conference with the aim of establishing a peace settlement. The demands from ELAS were considered too excessive, but the earlier 'percentages agreement' struck between Churchill and Stalin now bore fruit, as the Soviets decided to stay aloof from the issue and thereby allow ELAS to lose their advantage. A ceasefire was agreed on 15 January 1945, in return for the republicans withdrawing their troops and demobilising.

The final meeting of the original Big Three would be at their conference at Yalta, held between 4 and 11 February 1945 on the Crimean peninsula, on the shores of the Black Sea. Churchill and Roosevelt had already met on Malta a few days beforehand, but now they would join with Stalin to discuss further issues of major importance for the post-war world. With France and Belgium now fully liberated and the Allies moving across the borders of Germany, the end of the conflict was in sight. Yet each leader had his own priorities: Stalin wanted to bolster the Soviet Union's security by establishing political influence in Eastern Europe, in the same territories where Churchill was pushing for increased democracy, while Roosevelt sought

Crowds celebrating the re-establishment of the government of Greece, in a photograph taken on 14 January 1945 following the end of the country's short civil war. Among the many emblems carried by the crowd were these banners bearing the likeness of Churchill.

Churchill sits with the King of Saudi Arabia, Abdulaziz bin Abdul Rahman Al Saud, during lunch at Auberge due Lac, Fayoum in Egypt, in February 1945. An interpreter is standing behind the two leaders.

The Big Three photographed at the Yalta conference in February 1945, the last time they would meet in person. Standing behind the three leaders are, left to right: the British Foreign Secretary Anthony Eden; the American Secretary of State, Edward Stettinius; the British Permanent Under-Secretary of State for Foreign Affairs, Alexander Cadogan; the Soviet Commissar for Foreign Affairs, Vyacheslav Molotov; and the American Ambassador in Moscow, Averell Harriman.

Soviet support for the ongoing war against Japan.

To avoid another war breaking out in future, a spirit of greater co-operation between nations was agreed upon at Yalta which would lead to the creation of what eventually became the United Nations, an organisation devoted to maintaining international peace and security. The aims, structure and functionality of the new organisation were all discussed and largely resolved, with further discussions being held later on in Moscow. The UN Charter would finally be adopted on 25 June 1945, and enter into force in October.

The other urgent matter for the leaders to decide upon was the future of Poland. A somewhat uneasy compromise was reached, whereby the Soviet Union would retain much of the territory that it had taken over in 1939, but with the western Polish border extended accordingly into Germany. Over two million Poles were subsequently expelled by Stalin and forced to move to the west. Poland had already suffered greatly as a result of the war, losing around 6 million of its population; half of these were Jews who were killed as a result of the Nazi Holocaust and Soviet purges. Churchill faced strong criticism regarding the decisions made over Poland, although as the junior partner among the Big Three, he struggled under difficult circumstances.

A further controversial decision was the forced repatriation of Soviet citizens and prisoners of war back to the Soviet Union. While many of these were soldiers from the Red Army, others were Cossacks, Ukrainians or ethnic Russians who had fought for the Nazis, as well as refugees who had fled Russian territory years before to avoid persecution. During 1946 and 1947 these people would now be forcibly returned into Soviet hands, where they often ended up in gulag prisons and put to work under terrible conditions. As such, more recent assessments of the Yalta agreement have in hindsight regarded it as being a war crime under today's international law, since it violated individual human rights.

Other decisions supported during this time by Churchill have drawn similar criticism. Although the Allied advance towards Berlin was progressing well, there remained doubts as to whether the Soviets might still falter in the east, allowing a Nazi counter-attack. Assistance to the fighting on that front was therefore deemed a wise precaution to take, and the city of Dresden was considered a key target due to its location as a communications and transport hub. Aerial bombing might cause enough disruption to stop German reinforcements moving in from the west, and halt civilian evacuation from the east.

Around 1,200 British and German bombers attacked Dresden on the nights of 13–15 February 1945, causing massive devastation to the city. Modern estimates suggest that as many as 25,000 people were killed, including many refugees and casualties who had retreated there from the fighting further east. The indiscriminate nature of some of the bombing has since been heavily criticised, since the Allied raids killed roughly the same number of Soviet citizens as German ones. On 28 March, Churchill decided to call a halt to further area bombing campaigns and wrote to his Chiefs of Staff accordingly.

> The destruction of Dresden remains a serious query against the conduct of Allied bombing... I feel the need for more precise concentration upon military objectives... rather than on mere acts of terror and wanton destruction, however impressive.

Critics of Churchill have since pointed to this policy as an example of his heavy-handedness, yet it seems that he had the sincere aim of shortening the war and, when he realised the extent of casualties, did call a swift end to the campaign. In that regard, his decision to approve the policy in the first place perhaps reflects the similar decision by President Harry S Truman later that year to use atomic bombs against Japan. Yet the punishment inflicted on Dresden and other German cities meant that the resulting loss of life and devastation would be remembered long after the war had finished, tarnishing the reputation of the Bomber Command leaders, particular Air Chief Marshal Sir Arthur Harris, as well as Churchill.

The pressures of leadership can be great, and no more is this true than in the case of a war leader. But throughout the conflict Churchill had his wife Clementine to rely on, as his closest friend and confidante. Churchill was by all accounts far from an easy man to either work or live with, and Clementine's positive influence undoubtedly helped his relationships with both staff and colleagues. She remained a regular companion during his many travels, whether inspecting bomb damage, troops or factory workers, and took on roles in numerous wartime charities. Among the most notable of these initiatives was the Aid to Russia Fund, organised by the Red Cross, for which she raised a considerable amount of money. In recognition of this, towards the end of the war she was invited to tour the Soviet Union as a personal guest of Stalin, with the visit happening to coincide with the final moments of the Nazi regime. Victory was close at hand, and her Russian trip would rob her of the opportunity to be at her husband's side for Britain's first proper celebration of victory.

But the final moves of the war were still to be played out. The early morning of 24 March 1945 saw the British 21st Army Group lead the Allied crossing of the river Rhine, a great symbolic moment in which the Allies entered the German homeland proper. As commander of 21st Army Group, Field Marshal Bernard Montgomery hosted a visit from Churchill at his Tactical Headquarters shortly before the crossing operation:

> We have a friendly talk after tea. He is dressed as a Colonel of the 4th Hussars. I tell him he is junior to a field-marshal and must obey my orders the next day when a lot of shells will be flying about. He agrees!

Churchill's presence was two-fold: although ostensibly there to encourage the troops and boost morale, it was also characteristic of him to want to be at the centre of any action. Archie Allen was serving on the staff of the 3rd Division and recalls the encouragement they

Clementine Churchill inspects members of the Auxiliary Transport Service (ATS) at the Royal Artillery Experimental Unit, Shoeburyness, Essex in February 1943. Clementine undertook many such duties as the Prime Minister's wife.

Churchill steps ashore from an American Landing Craft (or Higgins boat) onto the east bank of the River Rhine, south of Wesel in Germany, on 25 March 1945.

received from their war leader:

> We crossed the River Maas and were waiting to cross the Rhine and into Germany, when we were visited by Winston Churchill himself, who addressed us as he sat on an armoured vehicle and told us we would 'teach the Nazis a lesson by driving into their country – never done before in this way'. Within a short time of his leaving we suffered a Mother and a Father of a shelling by German gunners.

Churchill was also unable to resist the opportunity to explore newly captured territory, as Montgomery recalled:

> On the day after the Rhine is crossed, the 25 March 1945, I take him and Eisenhower to a viewpoint from which to see the enemy side. He suggests we should go over and look around. All seems quiet. I agree. Eisenhower is not too happy about it, and departs. We cross in an American landing craft of Ninth US Army, which is under my command. He enjoys jokes with the crew during the crossing. We land on the German side, accompanied by a milling crowd of Press photographers and reporters – including one lady (not British!). We walk inland for a little way. There is some shelling in the distance and Wesel bridge, downstream from us, is under shell fire. I say we must go back. He suggests we should visit Wesel bridge. We return to our shore and drive by car to the bridge. He wants to walk on the destroyed bridge. I say 'No'. Finally I agree, unwillingly, as the shelling has ceased. He goes. He stands alone on the top of the debris in the centre of the bridge – which had been blown by the Germans. Some shells come over. I order him back. He obeys my order – unwillingly.
>
> Having got him off the destroyed bridge, I take him and the CIGS to have a picnic lunch on the bank of the Rhine – on our side, and downstream from Wesel. The tide of battle has now moved away eastwards and all is quiet along the great river.

Once the Allies began to push on into Germany towards Berlin, the end of the Second World War in Europe became inevitable. Mussolini had been captured by Italian partisans on 27 April and swiftly executed while Hitler, trapped in his bunker beneath Berlin, shot himself on 30 April to escape the same fate. Grand Admiral Karl Doenitz was appointed as Hitler's successor, but knew that any attempt to continue the war was doomed to failure. The Germans signed an act of military surrender on Monday, 7 May 1945 at Reims, with a full unconditional surrender to follow the next day. The good news was broadcast in Britain late on the Monday evening, including the announcement that the following day would be a public holiday to mark Victory in Europe, or VE Day.

After years of suffering from wartime restrictions, air raids and separation from loved ones, the population of Britain could finally park their troubles and think about celebrating. Colourful bunting and flags lined the streets of villages, towns and cities across Britain. Bonfires

THE PATH TO VICTORY

PREVIOUS PAGE Churchill, never one to be overly concerned about his own safety, looks over the Rhine from the ruins of the west end of the bridge at Wesel, 25 March 1945. He was hastily ushered to safety following the taking of this photograph.

Churchill photographed in the garden at No 10 Downing Street, alongside his Chiefs of Staff, on 7 May 1945. The German unconditional surrender had been signed that day. Shown seated, left to right, are Air Chief Marshal Sir Charles Portal; Field Marshal Sir Alan Brooke; Churchill; and Admiral Sir Andrew Cunningham. Standing behind are the Secretary to the Chiefs of Staffs Committee, Major General L C Hollis (left) and the Chief of Staff to the Minister of Defence, General Sir Hastings Ismay (right).

The Royal Family, accompanied by Churchill, wave to the crowds from the balcony of Buckingham Palace on the afternoon of VE Day, 8 May 1945.

Churchill at the microphone in the Cabinet Office making his VE Day broadcast to the nation to say that the war with Germany had been won, 8 May 1945.

Churchill acknowledges the cheers of the crowd on VE Day, 8 May 1945, from the balcony of the Ministry of Health building in Whitehall. Amongst those politicians present are Ernest Bevin (Minister of Labour, to the immediate left of Churchill); and Sir John Anderson (Chancellor of the Exchequer), Lord Woolton (Minister of Reconstruction) and Herbert Morrison (Minister of Home Security), all to the right of the Prime Minister.

were lit, people danced and the pubs were full of riotous laughter. Many made their way to London, the centre of the British Empire, to celebrate alongside their leaders – the Royal Family and British government – who had seen them through the conflict. In a moment that would forever capture Churchill's importance to Britain's victory over Nazi Germany, he appeared on the balcony of Buckingham Palace to greet the massive crowds below, alongside the King and Queen and royal princesses. Many were not anticipating the Prime Minister to be at the royal palace, since Whitehall was the more natural place to expect to see him appear to the crowds. Among the huge numbers making their way to this second location, in the hope of hearing the prime Minister speak, was Cynthia Edwards, a teacher from Putney:

> We went down Whitehall to Downing St but the police said Mr Churchill would be at the Ministry of Health, so we joined the huge gathering. We were told he was to appear at 5pm but we waited an hour and had just pushed to the back of the crowd because we could not stand the heat a moment longer, when suddenly at 10 to 6 the cheers grew louder and everyone rushed forward. We just managed to get back round the corner far enough to see him. The crowd cheered and cheered and cheered. At last he tried to speak, but had to stop two or three times because every time he uttered a syllable the crowd shouted, and whistled and clapped and rang bells and rattles and blew horns. At last he said 'God bless you all'. More cheers. Then he gave just a short unprepared speech which was interrupted by more cheers.
>
> 'This is your hour. This is not victory of a party or any class. It's a victory of the great British nation as a whole… The lights went out and the bombs came down. But every man, woman and child in the country had no thought of quitting the struggle.'

That same evening, Churchill's broadcast on the radio was heard by Clementine, many miles away in Moscow as a guest of Stalin:

> In the Embassy, I heard my husband's voice broadcasting from London the announcement for which the world had been waiting. M. Edouard Herriot, the great French statesman, and his wife, who had been recently liberated after many hardships and discomforts from their German captivity, were with us in Moscow. After the broadcast, M. Herriot said to me: 'I am afraid you may think it unmanly of me to weep. But I have just heard Mr Churchill's voice. The last time I had heard his voice was on that day in Tours in 1940 when he implored the French Government to hold firm and continue the struggle. His noble words of leadership that day were unavailing. When he heard the French Government's answer, and knew that they meant to give up the fight, tears streamed down Mr Churchill's face. So you will understand that if I weep today, I do not feel unmanned'.

Yet for those in the forces who were still serving overseas, or in captivity as prisoners of war, as well as relatives awaiting the return of their loved ones, VE Day proved to be a bittersweet moment. While victory had been achieved in what was, to those in Britain, the most important theatre of war, the conflict was continuing in the Far East and Pacific. In his radio broadcast that evening, Churchill promised that victory in the war against Japan would soon follow. But little could he ever have imagined that it would be another person leading the country at that time.

CHAPTER NINE
LIFE AFTER CONFLICT

With the war in Europe now over and the fighting against the Japanese in the Pacific appearing to move towards its end, the wartime coalition National government began to break up. Labour supporters condemned those compromises that their MPs, led by Deputy Prime Minister Clement Attlee, had been obliged to agree to as members of the coalition. A General Election was called for, since there had been no such democratic vote since well before the conflict began. Churchill therefore resigned on 23 May 1945 but continued as Prime Minister of a 'caretaker' National government formed mainly of Conservatives and Liberals.

Beginning on 17 July, he attended the last of the wartime conferences at Potsdam, in the Soviet-occupied sector of Germany. This was the first such international meeting at which the United States was represented by new President Harry S Truman, who had taken over following the death of Roosevelt three months earlier. Churchill and Roosevelt had enjoyed each other's company and forged a firm friendship; in his eulogy following the President's death, Churchill declared that in Roosevelt the United Kingdom had lost the greatest friend it had ever known. Yet discussions between the new Big Three would continue and cover in particular the administration of occupied Germany, which it had already agreed would be split into four zones controlled by the Soviets, Americans, British and French.

Churchill was accompanied to Potsdam by Foreign Secretary Anthony Eden and also by his election rival Clement Attlee. All expected Churchill to win the election, but evidence suggests that Churchill's mind was indeed still occupied by events back home; a degree of uncertainty about the future seems to have made itself known. Eden afterwards declared that he found Churchill's performance at the Potsdam conference to be disappointing, particularly by his acquiescing to Stalin's wishes regarding matters such as the administration of Poland. Montgomery also noted Churchill's different attitude:

> I saw a great deal of Churchill at Potsdam because as C-in-C and Military Governor of the British Zone of Germany I had to be at hand if wanted. He appeared to me to be restless and tired; things were not going the way he wanted; Stalin had fastened his grip very firmly on eastern Europe and was not going to give it up.

Churchill, Attlee and Eden would all return to Britain after nine days in order to receive the results of the General Election on 26 July. Although balloting was held on 5 July, the result had to be delayed for three weeks to allow the votes of those serving in the forces overseas to be counted. Among them was Lieutenant Denis Gudgeon in Bombay who, writing home to his family on 1 July 1945, was critical of what he had heard so far from Churchill:

> Have been listening to Churchill's election speeches on the wireless and was very disappointed by them. He seems to have lost interest

PREVIOUS PAGE In this photograph from Churchill's visit to the Netherlands in 1948, he and Queen Juliana look on as Juliana's daughter Irene holds her baby sister Marijke in her arms. Churchill was asked to be Marijke's godfather.

Churchill delivers his final address during the 1945 General Election campaign, at Walthamstow Stadium in East London.

and his arguments and reasoning are very feeble. I can't believe it's the same man talking after hearing some of his fighting speeches. He is definitely a Wartime Premier and don't consider him suitable for peacetime. I hope Stafford Cripps gets in, partly because the Russians like him. I am very much afraid we may have a war with the Russians in about 15 years time.

To the surprise of many, the Labour Party won the election with an absolute majority over all other parties, achieving one of the greatest landslide victories of modern British politics. But how was it that Churchill, the great war leader who had received such acclaim just two months earlier when victory in Europe was achieved, had now been given (in his own words) 'the order of the boot'? Many felt that Churchill had campaigned poorly, perhaps being over-confident due to his wartime reputation and concentrating on criticising the Labour Party rather than promoting his own policies. An ill-judged speech in which he accused Attlee of planning to use 'Gestapo' methods of government did nothing to help him, although arguably the most important factor was a widespread public desire for post-war social reform, something which had been particularly championed by Attlee's Labour Party as opposed to the somewhat half-hearted support for

An unusual photograph showing the set up of the conference room at Potsdam on 19 July 1945. Churchill can be seen at the top of the table, while Stalin sits at the four o'clock position and Truman at eight o'clock.

OPPOSITE Churchill and US President Harry Truman shake hands on the steps of Truman's residence 'The White House' at Kaiser Strasse in Babelsberg, Germany, on 16 July 1945. Franklin D Roosevelt had died in April, and this first meeting of Churchill with the new American leader was for the Potsdam conference.

LIFE AFTER CONFLICT

change declared by Churchill and the Conservatives.

Demands for a more egalitarian society had grown within Britain as the war progressed, while victory had now enabled such change to be a realistic possibility. A report commissioned by the government's Home Intelligence Division in November 1942 had found that most people in Britain wanted five main things after the war – a living wage for all workers; the good of the community being placed above profit; financial security for those unable to work; decent housing for all; and equality of access to education. A subsequent report issued soon after by economist William Beveridge set out a blueprint for post-war social policy which supported all these principles, adding the creation of a National Health Service and free medical care.

But while the Beveridge Report received widespread public support for its post-war vision, Churchill's reaction was rather half-hearted. He considered some of its aims unrealistic to achieve, and talked only of a muddled 'four year plan' which lacked proper detail. Preferring to concentrate on the military aspects of the war and in particular maintenance of the Grand Alliance, Churchill would regularly pass questions of domestic policy to his wartime Deputy, Clement Attlee, to deal with. It is therefore no surprise that it was Attlee and the Labour Party that became so closely associated with supporting this post-war vision. Some research has suggested that voters may have welcomed Churchill staying on as prime minister while rejecting the policies of his Conservative Party, but the two things came as a package. Churchill won his own parliamentary seat comfortably, yet was no longer Prime Minster and had to take up a new role as Leader of the Opposition.

Japan announced its surrender on 15 August 1945, with the Second World War coming to a formal close on 2 September with Attlee as the new British Prime Minister. But although no longer leader, Churchill was still seen as the man who had led Britain to victory in the war. His reputation remained particularly high in the United States and he received many invitations to speak there. The invitation he finally chose to accept was from Westminster College in Fulton, Missouri, which came with a supportive note from the US President Harry Truman imploring him to accept. On 5 March 1946, reporters from all over the world gathered in Westminster College's gymnasium to witness Churchill receive an honorary degree and deliver what would become known as his 'Sinews of Peace' address. With Truman at his side, Churchill talked about the post-war balance of power:

> A shadow has fallen upon the scenes so lately lighted by the Allied victory. Nobody knows what Soviet Russia and its Communist international organisation intends to do in the immediate future, or what are the limits, if any, to their expansive and proselytising tendencies. I have a strong admiration and regard for the valiant Russian people and for my wartime comrade, Marshal Stalin. There is deep sympathy and goodwill in Britain – and I doubt not here also – towards the peoples of all the Russias... It is my duty however... to place before you certain facts about the present position in Europe.

OPPOSITE A General Election poster from 1945, encouraging support for Churchill to 'finish the job', linking his successful wartime leadership with the need for post-war recovery and reconstruction. The British public remained unconvinced and the result was a Labour landslide.

> From Stettin in the Baltic to Trieste in the Adriatic, an iron curtain has descended across the Continent. Behind that line lie all the capitals of the ancient states of Central and Eastern Europe. Warsaw, Berlin, Prague, Vienna, Budapest, Belgrade, Bucharest and Sofia, all these famous cities and the populations around them lie in what I must call the Soviet sphere... The Communist parties, which were very small in all these Eastern States of Europe, have been raised to pre-eminence and power far beyond their numbers and are seeking everywhere to obtain totalitarian control. Police governments are prevailing in nearly every case, and so far, except in Czechoslovakia, there is no true democracy.

OPPOSITE Churchill speaks at Westminster College in Fulton, Missouri on 5 March 1946. This was the speech in which he referred to an 'Iron Curtain' resulting from the Soviet occupation of much of eastern Europe.

While Churchill's reference to an 'iron curtain' was not the first use of such a phrase, either by him or others, the Fulton speech was certainly the moment when it was adopted widely and began to enter common parlance as a representation of the political and ideological boundary now separating Europe. Indeed, this moment of Churchill identifying the separate alliances on each side of the 'curtain' has since been regarded as marking the beginning of what would become known as the Cold War.

Churchill's attitude towards communism and the Soviet Union was particularly well-received in the United States, where many people struggled to understand why he had been voted out of office in Britain the previous year. Dorothy Morrison wrote from Miami to a friend in Britain on 3 June 1946, shortly after Churchill's Fulton address:

> I was so relieved in reading your last letter to know that you felt as I do about Churchill. How could the masses throw him out for someone they know nothing about! Was it because of the promises that Attlee made in his election speeches – or just a desire for a change – or is it part of this octopus... which is undermining our country too – reaching out from Moscow? I positively get cold chills when I listened to Churchill's address on the air in Missouri in which he underlined the menace that throws its shadow around the world – but I am with him 100% and personally I think if the USA and Great Britain don't hang together they will hang separately! Churchill made a tremendous hit here. Everyone concedes the fact that he is one of, if not the great man of our age. I admire him no end.

The immediate post-war period saw Churchill basking in fame, and his financial situation improved as a result. For somebody commonly regarded as a reliable figure of stability, Churchill had struggled with his personal finances throughout his life and was frequently in serious debt, largely due to the lavish lifestyle that he was used to enjoying as a member of the aristocracy. One of the main elements of this extravagance was alcohol, on which Churchill spent a staggering amount of money, not only in terms of the quantity he consumed but also the quality; his bills from wine merchants or restaurants were frequently huge. He was also a keen gambler and could rarely resist the opportunity to indulge, whether in casinos or privately between friends, and also gambled on the stock market. Churchill's fascination with new innovations led to regular investment in such things as oilfields, electricity, gas and rolling stock.

This extravagant spending, combined with significant financial losses as a result of the Wall Street Crash in 1929, had meant that Churchill's money had effectively run out by the beginning of the war. He had been forced to put Chartwell and his London home on the market at that point, but by remarkable good fortune a rich benefactor stepped in to pay off a good deal of the debts in a secret show of support for his stance against Hitler. And now Churchill's improved status after the war brought with it many further opportunities to make money, whether by selling film rights to his various books, or through public speaking. Most notably, a group of friends and admirers contributed to a fund to purchase Chartwell on behalf of the National Trust, who rented the property back to the Churchill family for a nominal amount.

No longer in danger of bankruptcy, Churchill could continue to spend excessively during the final years of his life, but now with much less worry. He maintained an expensive body of staff who accompanied him on his regular travels overseas, and would always stay in luxury hotels, mix with the elite of society and eat and drink the very best. With the immediate stresses of war and leadership having been removed from his shoulders, his health improved too. Apart from a hernia operation in 1947 and a few bad colds, his energy and enthusiasm impressed all who met him.

It was expected that he would bring this sense of energy to the first Council of Europe meeting in Strasbourg, scheduled for August 1949. Churchill firmly supported this organisation, formed to uphold democracy, human rights and the rule of law in Europe after the war. Although no longer a head of state, he remained one of the main instigators of greater support among the European democracies to bolster against the threat from communism. Yet although speaking in favour of the Council, and having earlier advocated 'a kind of United States of Europe' in remedy to the tragic state in which the Second World War had left the continent, he regarded Europe more as a counter to Soviet Russia rather than a unified group for its own sake. Churchill was most concerned with wanting to see past glories restored, amidst assured peace and prosperity. France and Germany in particular would need to work closely together, while Britain would remain in a role as one of the influential supporters of this 'new' Europe.

Before arriving at Strasbourg for the meeting, Churchill decided to spend a few days at Lord Beaverbrook's villa in the south of France. But after staying up until two in the morning, playing gin rummy and sustained by many cigars and much alcohol, he suffered a second stroke. Churchill's health problems remained a closely guarded secret, and he refused to confine himself to extensive rest; he therefore proceeded to attend the first session of the Council a day or two later. But the incident served as a reminder that (at the age of 74) he was

no longer a young man, and further health concerns would make themselves known over the following few years.

The first signs that Churchill might be able to regain political power once more came with the General Election of 23 February 1950, which Labour again won but this time with a greatly reduced majority of just five seats. The government called a snap election on 25 October the following year in an attempt to increase its parliamentary majority, yet failed to do so; the Conservatives achieved a majority of 17 seats and therefore were able to form a new government, with Churchill restored as Prime Minister. He received a personal record of almost 41,000 votes in his constituency of Woodford. The Labour election campaign had been weakened by schisms between the party's Right and Left, while the Conservatives had fought hard to re-establish themselves as a credible return to prosperity, with Churchill's charisma proving essential to their success. He received particular praise for a radio broadcast in which he described the difference between the Conservative and Labour outlooks as being respectively 'on the ladder' to prosperity or 'in the queue' to nothing. For the 76-year-old Churchill, it was a chance to put his defeat in 1945 to rest for good, and to embrace a final opportunity to lead the United Kingdom.

To begin with, it seemed that Churchill was emulating the formation of his wartime Cabinet, appointing Anthony Eden once again as Foreign Secretary and initially himself as Minister of Defence. Indeed, Churchill's main preoccupation throughout his second period as Prime Minister remained foreign affairs. Fully aware of international tension and the potential for nuclear war, he regarded co-operation between nations as the best option to maintain peace and sought to strengthen the 'special relationship' between the United States and Britain, just as he had done during the war years. Yet the several transatlantic flights he took to meet with Presidents Truman and Eisenhower were not necessarily as fruitful as the meetings he had enjoyed with their predecessor, Roosevelt. The leaders struggled to reach agreements over a number of important issues, not least American military commitments in West Germany and the Middle East.

One of the problems faced by Churchill was that he did not realise that Britain was now a more junior player on the world stage, reliant on America's greater influence. He believed that retaining the British Empire remained crucial for Britain to consider itself a world power, yet the policy of decolonisation which had immediately followed the war was slowly dismantling this. Churchill was particularly disappointed to have to accept the evacuation of British troops from Suez in October 1954, following the establishment of Colonel Nasser's new government in Egypt two years earlier. In addition, the Malayan Emergency, which had begun in 1948 when communist guerrilla fighters started an uprising against British and Commonwealth troops, remained an ongoing issue, as did the similar Mau Mau uprising in British Kenya from 1952.

Much of the Churchill government's domestic affairs were left to Harold Macmillan to deal with, as the Minister of Housing and

PREVIOUS PAGE 'Looking fit and bronzed', according to the original wartime caption, Churchill arrives at Hendon airport on 5 October 1945 to be met by Clementine. He was returning from a continental holiday, during which he had lost some £7,000 at the Monte Carlo casinos. But his personal finances would improve in subsequent years, largely due to his wartime reputation.

OPPOSITE Bust of Churchill by Jacob Epstein, 1947. Although commissioned in late August 1945, shortly after Churchill's election defeat in July that year, Churchill was not available for sitting until the winter of 1946–47.

Local government. Some progress was made in demolishing slums and building new homes, and the Conservative manifesto promise of constructing 300,000 new homes each year was easily met. Yet housing was one of the few aspects of home affairs that Churchill took a particular interest in.

Poor health revisited Churchill throughout this second premiership. By now he had reached his eighties and was considerably past the age at which most people retire, yet was leading the country and facing stresses and burdens under which even a younger person might struggle. His health remained a constant worry, with even the King expressing concern at Churchill's wellbeing before passing away himself in February 1952. The common belief held by senior Conservatives was that Churchill only intended to stay in office for a few months before handing power over to Anthony Eden, whom most regarded as his natural successor. Yet Eden was suffering from his own health problems, and Churchill's inclination seemed to be to hold on to power for as long as he could. A certain rivalry therefore existed between Churchill, Eden and Macmillan, which added another element of complication to any key decision making.

April 1953 would see Churchill finally receive his knighthood. Immediately after the war he had been offered the Order of the Garter, the highest British civilian or military honour. Yet he had felt reluctant to accept it at that time due to having just been voted out of office at the 1945 General Election. It seemed that the country no longer required his services, making such an award appear more as a concession rather than a true honour. But his return as Prime Minister now made the situation rather different, and when offered the honour again by the new Queen Elizabeth II, he swiftly accepted. Knighted on 24 April, it would therefore be *Sir* Winston Churchill in attendance at the coronation on 2 June that same year.

The coronation proved to be the grandest public celebration since the end of the war, and a population used to austerity embraced the opportunity with vigour. Churchill's love for pageantry and ceremony was well-suited to organising the extraordinary event, and his influence extended from deciding upon the arrangement of the formal processions and appropriate dress for members of his Cabinet, to the choice of national anthems to be played at Westminster Abbey. His own attendance was greeted warmly by the watching crowds, yet his jovial manner perhaps hid the stress which he had recently been experiencing. Preparing for the coronation had caused enough exertion, but he had also had to attend the conference of Commonwealth Prime Ministers and been effectively running the Foreign Office while Anthony Eden was absent due to illness.

Churchill had suffered another minor stroke in February 1952, but a more serious one occurred in June 1953 just weeks after the coronation, at a party at Downing Street. Despite attempts to hide his health problems from the public, it was becoming very obvious that age was getting the better of Churchill. He had also been suffering from hearing problems since the war, and relied on a walking stick on occasion. His cognitive ability was now becoming noticeably worse, likely due to the series of minor strokes he had suffered, yet as ever he would continue to surprise his doctors with his endless energy.

Aside from politics, Churchill remained fully occupied during the post-war period with his many writings. He produced an enormous body of literature throughout his long life, and his memoirs of the Second World War filled six volumes that began to appear from 1948. Churchill's influential wartime speeches were also published to great acclaim, and it was almost certainly this element of his writing that led to his award of the Nobel Prize for Literature in October 1953. Churchill was attending an international conference in Bermuda at the time of the Nobel ceremony, and so Clementine visited Stockholm to accept the award on her husband's behalf. Churchill was allegedly somewhat disappointed with the award, as he had hopes of receiving the more important Nobel Peace Prize instead, but the Prize for Literature was indeed extraordinary and served as a fine tribute to his impressive output. Perhaps the Prize inspired his next great series of books, which would cover the earlier period of British history up to 1900 – *A History of the English-Speaking Peoples* – the first volume of which would be published in 1956.

But Churchill knew himself that he was slowing down both mentally and physically, and it was only right that he should finally step aside as Prime Minister. He therefore resigned on 5 April 1955 and handed over power to Anthony Eden.

CHAPTER TEN
CHURCHILL'S LEGACY

After stepping down as Prime Minister, Churchill continued as a Member of Parliament, although his involvement in political matters became much less as time went on. His attendance at the House of Commons was sporadic at best and he continued to have regular health scares, as recalled by his frequent visitor Bernard Montgomery:

> Towards the end of September 1957 he became very ill with pneumonia while at Roquebrune. He recovered and [I visited him] on 12 October; he was then convalescing and could sit out in the sun. He looked in pretty good form and was painting a good deal. I sat with him for long periods and got him to talk of his experiences in South Africa, the Sudan, and the Indian Frontier. He was now 83 years old and, though obviously delicate and needing great care, there was no apparent sign that he was beginning to go 'downhill'. And his brain was active and alert. But he did get easily tired, and he now began to stay in bed until about 12 noon, getting up for lunch.

By the time of the 1959 General Election, Churchill was rarely to be seen in Parliament. This lack of engagement almost surely explains why his constituency vote at Woodford fell by more than a thousand, his continued status as an MP now depending solely on his wartime reputation rather than any current talents. He did, however, easily retain the title of 'Father of the House', an honorary designation in the House of Commons awarded to the Member of Parliament who could claim the longest continuous service. Aware that the population of Woodford may well be ready to choose a more dynamic candidate to represent them, Churchill finally decided to step down as an MP shortly before the next General Election. He left the House of Commons for the very last time on 27 July 1964.

This gradual disconnection with politics allowed Churchill to begin to live a more retiring lifestyle, spending much of his time at Chartwell or his London home at Hyde Park Gate. His fondness for socialising and holidaying abroad continued, however, with the south of France being a particularly favourite location where he could make full use of the high-class hotels and casinos. He continued to mix with the rich elite of society, and in 1959 embarked on a Mediterranean cruise onboard the personal yacht of the millionaire Aristotle Onassis. A regular visitor to Monaco, Churchill would spend thousands of pounds gambling, in spite of Clementine's disapproval.

When staying in Monte Carlo in June 1962, Churchill fell out of bed and broke his hip, leading to his having to be flown back to Britain for medical treatment at the insistence of the current Prime Minister, Harold Macmillan. Macmillan was concerned that Churchill might die while in France, which would be seen as 'inappropriate' for such a British hero. This unpleasant incident appears to have had a profound effect on Churchill's confidence, making him take a step back from his usual excesses. Churchill's health became a particular concern to his old friend Bernard Montgomery, who recorded how the accident had

PREVIOUS PAGE The State Funeral of Sir Winston Churchill on 30 January 1965. Churchill's coffin, borne on a gun carriage pulled by a detachment from the Royal Navy, is escorted by officers of the RAF as it moves up Whitehall and passes the Cenotaph, heading towards Trafalgar Square. Crowds line the street to pay their respects.

OPPOSITE Churchill in his study, October 1951. A prodigious writer, he received much praise for his *History of the Second World War* which was published between 1948 and 1953. Following a final stint as Prime Minister, Churchill then devoted much of his time to writing one last series of four books, *A History of the English-Speaking Peoples*.

A Churchill family portrait taken on the Pink Terrace at Chartwell in October 1951, showing, left to right, his daughter Diana (with husband Duncan Sandys and their son Julian); grandchildren Emma and Nicolas Soames and Winston Churchill Jr; wife Clementine with their granddaughter Arabella Churchill; and son Randolph.

affected his old comrade:

> I visited him in hospital and it was very clear to me that he would never be the same again. He recovered, and even took his place in the House of Commons. But knowing him as I did, I realised that he had begun to go downhill. It was now merely a question of how long the downhill decline would last. He went to the south of France early in 1963, and did a cruise in the yacht of Mr Onassis. But he got no better physically or mentally. From now onwards he was in [the] charge of four nurses, one male nurse and three women.

These final years of semi-retirement saw Churchill receive many tributes and awards, amongst the most notable being Citizenship of the United States, which was granted to him by President John F Kennedy on 9 April 1963. No longer fit enough to make the transatlantic flight, Churchill watched the ceremony on television from his London home, transmitted live via satellite from Washington DC where several hundred guests had gathered in the White House gardens. The distinction was accepted on Churchill's behalf by his son, Randolph.

Churchill suffered another, this time final, stroke at his home in Hyde Park Gate on 10 January 1965. He died there exactly two weeks later, in the early morning of 24 January, at the age of ninety. By curious coincidence, it happened to be the exact same day on which his father Randolph had died, some seventy years before. The BBC broadcast news of Churchill's death at 9am that morning, before playing a recording of Beethoven's Fifth Symphony, the opening theme of which emphasises three short notes followed by a long one – the letter 'V' in Morse code.

Plans for Churchill's funeral now began to be put into operation. Codenamed 'Operation Hope Not', the plans had begun to be formulated some years before, in 1953, when Churchill had suffered a serious stroke and it was feared that he might not have many more years left. As fate would have it, Churchill lived on for over a decade and therefore the funeral plan needed constant revision; as Lord Mountbatten put it, despite everybody's expectations Churchill continually managed to outlive his pallbearers. The Queen's decree that Churchill's funeral should be 'on a scale befitting his position in history' meant that he would be given the honour of a State Funeral, the sort of grand tribute usually reserved for monarchs but on very rare occasions granted to others who it was felt had earned such elevated recognition. Churchill's longevity allowed for constant revision of the funeral plans, and he even contributed to them himself. Montgomery noted at Christmas 1963 how it was:

> Significant that [Churchill's] secretarial staff have begun work on his funeral arrangements and there is a large and growing file on the subject at 28 Hyde Park Gate… He suddenly announced one day that he wished to be buried with his parents at Bladon, and not in Westminster Abbey nor in St Paul's. He was told that if he wished it thus he must record it in writing with his will, and this has been done. I

The State Funeral of Sir Winston Churchill on 30 January 1965. The cortege makes its way along Whitehall and passes the entrance to Downing Street.

CHURCHILL'S LEGACY

Churchill's coffin, draped with the Union Flag and carrying the insignia of a Knight of the Garter, is carried up the west steps of St Paul's Cathedral by eight Grenadier Guardsmen pallbearers, 30 January 1965.

am to be a Pall Bearer, by his special wish.

Churchill had earlier claimed to have wanted to be buried at Chartwell under the croquet lawn, and on another occasion for his ashes to be scattered alongside the graves of his various pet dogs. His longevity also meant that he had input into the guest list, objecting to the presence of French leader Charles de Gaulle, whom he disliked and mistrusted despite his status as a fellow Allied leader. He eventually acquiesced to de Gaulle being invited to the funeral for political reasons, yet insisted on a more circuitous route for the funeral procession via Waterloo Station, in the hope of forcing de Gaulle to have to walk bare-headed beneath the Waterloo archway, which signified Britain's famous past victory over France.

Implemented by the Duke of Norfolk, the elaborate funeral plan was put into operation as soon as news of Churchill's death was known. His body lay in state in Westminster Hall in London for three days from 27 January, to be viewed by over 321,000 mourners, and the state funeral was then scheduled for Saturday, 30 January 1965. The event was televised and would be witnessed by an estimated 350 million people worldwide, making it by far the largest funeral of its kind so far in British history.

The funeral procession began to make its way from Westminster Hall towards St Paul's Cathedral at 9.45am on the Saturday morning, as a ninety gun salute was fired from Hyde Park, marking the number of years of Churchill's life. The coffin, draped in a Union Flag, was pulled on a gun carriage and followed by male members of the Churchill family on foot, with Clementine and her two daughters following by coach. The marching band of the 2nd Battalion Scots Guards accompanied the procession, which in total consisted of some 2,500 soldiers and civilians, plus many more troops lining the route. The coffin arrived at St Paul's and was carried inside the cathedral by eight pallbearers, preceded by twelve honorary pallbearers who included former British Prime Ministers Clement Attlee, Anthony Eden and Harold Macmillan; the Prime Minister of Australia, Robert Menzies; and Admiral of the Fleet, Lord Louis Mountbatten. Montgomery had been unable to attend the funeral, due to health reasons.

The funeral service itself saw an enormous gathering of 3,500 invited mourners including dignitaries from more than 112 countries. Among the most notable were the French President Charles de Gaulle, the Prime Ministers of Canada and Rhodesia (now Zimbabwe), and former US President, Dwight D Eisenhower. Queen Elizabeth II broke royal protocol by attending the funeral of a non-royal, arriving at the cathedral before the coffin and Churchill's family – normally, a monarch would be the final person to arrive at such a ceremony. She also granted precedence to the family by insisting that they leave before herself.

Afterwards, the coffin was carried by Grenadier Guardsmen to the Tower Of London, from where it was taken on board a launch and along the Thames to Festival Pier. As the vessel passed, cranes along Hays

Wharf on the south bank of the river were lowered as a mark of respect. The coffin was then taken by hearse to Waterloo station, and loaded onto a special funeral train to transport it to Handborough, the nearest station to Bladon. The engine chosen for this important job was Southern Railway's locomotive 34051, one of forty-four 'Battle of Britain' class trains built immediately after the war. These were each named in tribute to aircraft or people involved in the defining battle and appropriately, the engine chosen for the funeral was the *Winston Churchill*. As the funeral train made its way to its final destination, thousands of sightseers lined the route to pay their final respects. Many military veterans stood to attention as the locomotive passed, saluting their war leader, while others were keen to simply snatch a glimpse of such an historical moment.

Finally, a private family service was held at St Martin's Church in Bladon, with Churchill's grave bearing two wreaths: one from Clementine, and the other from the Queen. He was laid to rest in the family plot alongside his parents, his brother Jack and daughter Diana, who had taken her own life only two years previously. Tens of thousands of people queued to see Churchill's final resting place to pay their respects over the following few days.

As the mourners drifted away and everyday life continued, it seemed that the era of Sir Winston Churchill, the last of the great Edwardian statesmen and veteran of two World Wars, was finally over. Tributes to him would continue to appear over the following decades, the most common being statues such as the striking example by Ivor Roberts-Jones installed in Parliament Square in London, overlooking the Houses of Parliament where Churchill spent so much of his time. Churchill's name had already been given to the College at the University of Cambridge that now houses his extensive archive of personal papers.

Perhaps Churchill's greatest legacy was his reputation. While many today might remain ignorant of his specific roles and conduct, and indeed may question the wisdom of some of his beliefs and statements, the name and image of Churchill remains well-known and surely will forever be associated with the qualities of integrity, strength and stoicism. While the man himself may not have reached the heights of human perfection that some ascribe to him, he will most likely be remembered long into the future as personifying those impressive qualities. The role that he played in ensuring that Britain and her Allies achieved victory over Nazi Germany and its allies in the Second World War is undeniable. As somebody who always believed that he had a special role to play in his nation's history, that legacy is therefore wholly appropriate.

This Second World War decorative horse-brass bears the profile of Churchill and is typical of the many pieces of 'Churchilliana' commissioned both during the war and afterwards, based on his image. The design includes his familiar cigar as well as a reference to Churchill's characteristically defiant 'V' for Victory gesture.

Churchill's strong image and memorable personality mean that he is regularly associated with many different commercial products. The selection shown here includes whisky, cocktails and a cookbook, reflecting his love for quality food and drink, while his famous quotes frequently adorn mugs and numerous other souvenirs.

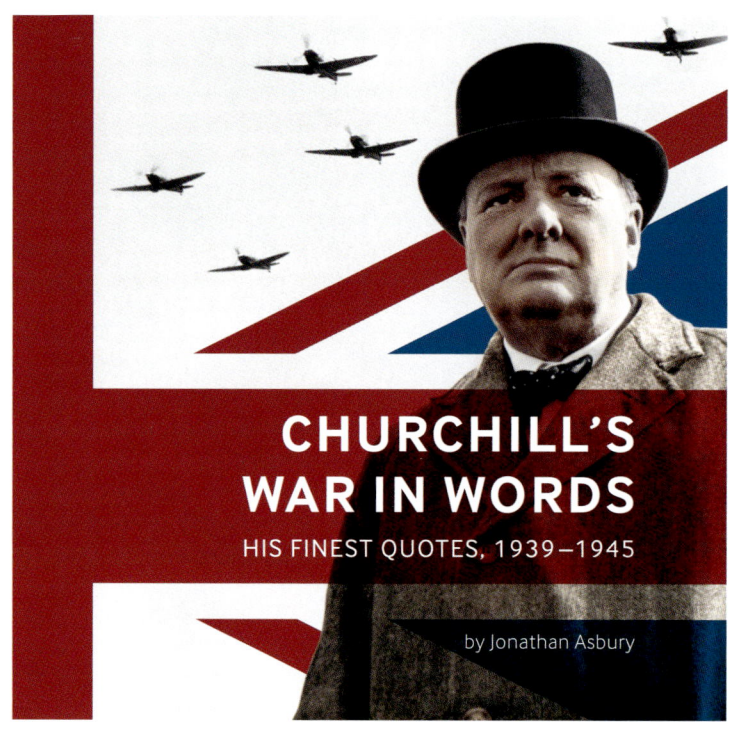

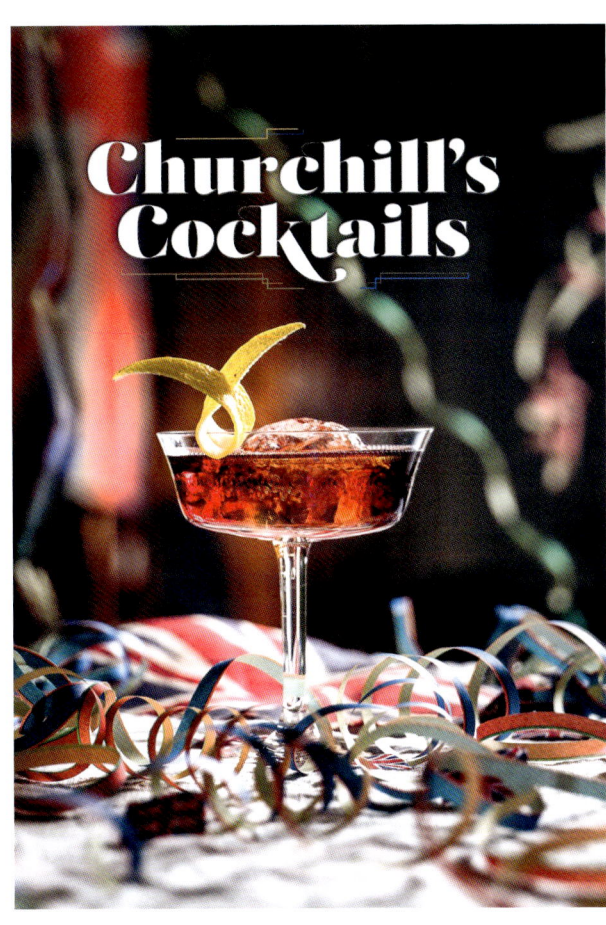

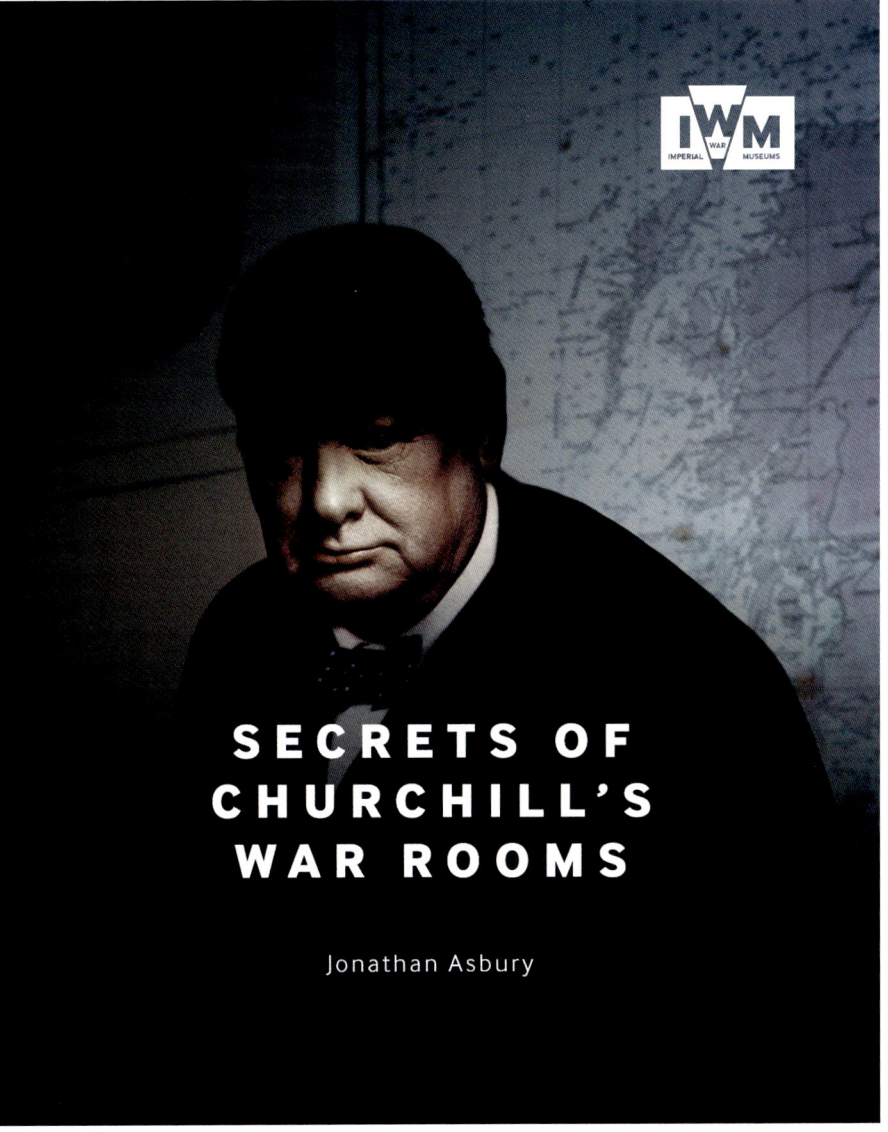

SOURCES

IWM Documents © IWM unless otherwise stated
Private Papers of A Allen (Documents.18934) © A Allen
Private Papers of Major General Sir Alec Bishop (Documents.7875) © The Rights Holder
Private Papers of D J Cooper (Documents.13049)
Private Paper of F S Davies (Documents.11626) © D M Davies
Private Papers of Miss C Edwards (Documents.25294)
Private Papers of Lieutenant F E Goldsworthy RNVR (Documents.18312) © The Rights Holder
Private Papers of Mrs Y M D Green (Documents.7929) © A Share-Kissiov & S Nichol
Private Papers of Lieutenant D G F Gudgeon (Documents.3527)
Private Papers of Lieutenant Colonel C E L Lyne (Documents.4746) © The Rights Holder
Private Papers of N Macleod (Documents.13607) © The Rights Holder
Private Papers of Lieutenant Commander E B Rhead DSC RNR (Documents.8112)
Private Papers of Captain R C Thorogood (Documents.26094)
Documents.16175 Reproduced with permission of Curtis Brown, London on behalf of The Estate of Sir Winston S Churchill © The Estate of Winston S Churchill
Documents.20501 Reproduced with permission of Henry Montgomery and Arabella Stuart-Smith

IWM Sound Archive © IWM unless otherwise stated
Gilbert Adshead (660)
Leonard Clark (13286)
Ellen Harris (9820)
Albert Masters (720)
Ivo Vesey (18564)

Other
Hansard: HC Debate 7 May 1940, 13 May 1940, 4 June 1940, 18 June 1940, 20 August 1940
Churchill, Winston, 'We will endeavour etc.' quoted by Duranti, Marco, *The Conservative Human Rights Revolution: European Identity, Transnational Politics, and the Origins of the European Convention* (Oxford University Press, 2017) Reproduced with permission of Curtis Brown, London on behalf of Sir Winston S Churchill © The Estate of Winston S Churchill
Churchill, Winston, 'The destruction of Dresden etc.' Quoted by Taylor, Frederick, *Dresden: Tuesday 13 February 1945* (Bloomsbury, 2005) Reproduced with permission of Curtis Brown, London on behalf of The Estate of Sir Winston S Churchill © The Estate of Winston S Churchill
Churchill, Winston, *My Early Life* (Thornton Butterworth, 1930) Reprinted by permission of Eland Publishing Ltd & with permission of Curtis Brown, London on behalf of The Estate of Sir Winston S Churchill © The Estate of Winston S Churchill
Churchill, Winston, *Thoughts and Adventures* (Thornton Butterworth, 1932) Reproduced with permission of Curtis Brown, London on behalf of The Estate of Sir Winston S Churchill © The Estate of Winston S Churchill
Churchill, Winston, 'Some chicken, some neck!' speech, 30 December 1941 Reproduced with permission of Curtis Brown, London on behalf of The Estate of Sir Winston S Churchill © The Estate of Winston S Churchill
Churchill, Winston, 'End of the beginning' speech, 10 November 1942 Reproduced with permission of Curtis Brown, London on behalf of The Estate of Sir Winston S Churchill © The Estate of Winston S Churchill
Churchill, Winston, 'This is your hour', 8 May 1945 Reproduced with permission of Curtis Brown, London on behalf of The Estate of Sir Winston S Churchill © The Estate of Winston S Churchill
Churchill, Winston, 'The Sinews of Peace' speech, 5 March 1946 Reproduced with permission of Curtis Brown, London on behalf of The Estate of Sir Winston S Churchill © The Estate of Winston S Churchill
Letter from George VI to Churchill, 2 June 1944, CHAR 20/136/4, Churchill Archives Centre, Reproduced with permission of Curtis Brown, London on behalf of The Estate of Sir Winston S Churchill © The Estate of Winston S Churchill

IMAGE LIST

All images supplied by IWM unless otherwise stated

Introduction 7 © The Rights Holder (Art.IWM ART 16839), 8 EPH 1406, 9 t NA 11797 b CI 678, 10 Art.IWM PST 3738, Chapter One 12 HU 98777, 15 ZZZ 7555D, 17 © The Print Collector / Alamy Stock Photo RC5P55, 18 l © Freemantle / Alamy Stock Photo RC667N r © Pictorial Press Ltd / Alamy Stock Photo CW2T7B, 20 t ZZZ 5426F b Q 72131, 21 FIR 10915, 23 ZZZ 7150D, 25 DC 731, Chapter Two 26 Q 81488, 29 Q 113382, 31 t Q 42037 b © Chronicle / Alamy Stock Photo A30NHA, 33 Q 107105, 36 Q 81835, Chapter Three 36 HU 55578, 41 EPH 9363, 42 CH 4779, 44 © Norman Wilkinson Estate. All rights reserved, DACS 2024 (Art.IWM ART 2450), 48 HU 129594, 49 FIR 3681, 50 Q 58127, 52 Q 49305, 55 Q 84077, 56 Art.IWM ART 1122, 58 Q 11428, Chapter Four 62 Q 81859, 65 Q 34718, 66 Q 34662, 67 Q 54941, 69 Q 66472E, 70 Q 103038, 71 Q 60172, 72 Q 107751, 74 © The Rights Holder (Art.IWM ART 5905), 77 Q 20578, Chapter Five 80 © Freemantle / Alamy Stock Photo 2K1R4WR, 84 © Sueddeutsche Zeitung Photo / Alamy Stock Photo C45H71, 86 HU 102771, 88 HU 4578, 89 NYP 68066, 91 HU 5547, Chapter Six 92 COL 30, 95 HU 73115, 96 H 10481, 99 HU 58256, 101 MH 26392, 102 H 2270, 104 H 4985, 106 Art.IWM PST 0761, 107 Art.IWM PST 4073, 108 H 10874, 109 H 14250, 110 H 14259, 111 H 31391, 113 COM 1076, 114 Reproduced with permission of Curtis Brown, London on behalf of The Estate of Sir Winston S. Churchill © The Estate of Winston S. Churchill (Documents.92), 115 IWM SITE CWR 000598, 116 IWM SITE CWR 000587, 117 IWM SITE CWR 000591, 118 IWM SITE CWR 000499, 120 H 4367, 121 HU 63613, 122 A 6900, 123 NY 7793, 125 H 25966, Chapter Seven 126 H 36960, 129 CAN 578, 130 Art.IWM PST 8063, 131 Art.IWM PST 3108, 133 (MOI) FLM 1117, 134 ME(RAF) 5060, 137 H 25955, 138 NA 474, 139 CNA 864, 140 A 19208, 142 E 26634, 143 E 26640, 144 K 5870, 145 © Transport for London (Art.IWM PST 6074), 147 CH 2903, 148 TR 1505, Chapter Eight 150 TR 2045, 153 B 5373, 154 B 7881, 155 B 8766, 157 H 41067, 158 Art.IWM PST 14383, 160 TR 2279, 161 OWIL 30645, 162 NA 17915, 163 BU 1292, 164 NA 21600, 165 MEM 2179, 167 TR 2828, 170 TR 682, 171 BU 2249, 173 EA 59831, 174 TR 2842, 175 MH 21835, 176 H 41844, 177 © The Rights Holder (HU 86145), Chapter Nine 180 © The Rights Holder (HU 52420), 183 HU 59722, 184 BU 8944, 185 BU 8986, 186 Art.IWM PST 8449, 188 © PA Images / Alamy G55ETM, 191 CH 16454, 192 Art.IWM ART LD 5851 © The Estate of Jacob Epstein / Tate, Chapter Ten 196 RAF-T 5117, 199 © The Rights Holder (HU 102863), 200 HU 102864, 202 RAF-T 5119, 204 RAF-T 5127, 207 © The Rights Holder (Art.IWM MED 1044), 208 FD00396, HW00955.

ACKNOWLEDGEMENTS

Sincere thanks to all those readers of the Visual History series, of which this is now the fourth volume. These books have provided us with a great opportunity to showcase some of the very best collections from IWM's vast archive and we remain extremely grateful to the contributors and rights holders for allowing us to present this wealth of testimony and illustrations. Thanks should also go to Phil Reed, my co-author on a previous Churchill book, for his many fascinating insights into Churchill's character which undoubtedly informed a lot of my writing. Also to James Taylor for his much-appreciated historical advice and checking of the text (any errors remaining are my own). The Visual History series is very much a team project which relies on many different people, but special thanks go to the IWM Publishing team (David, Maddy and Lara), our designer Georgia, who has made the layout look so wonderful, and all my other IWM colleagues across many teams who have made this book possible.

INDEX

Page numbers in *italics* refer to illustration captions

A

Admiral Graf Spee (cruiser) 94
Admiralty 37, 40–3, *42*, 46–7, 68, *90*, 94
Adshead, Gilbert 40, 43
Aid to Russia Fund, Red Cross 169
Alexander, General Sir Harold 136, *160*, 162
Aliens (Prevention of Crime) Bill 37
Allen, Archie 169, 172
Allied campaigns (1940–1945)
  France 152–9, *152*, *154*, *156*
  Germany 168–9, *171*, 172, *174*
  Italy 139, *160*, *162*
  North Africa 128, 132, *135*, 136, *139*
Altmark (tanker) 94
America *see* United States (US)
Amery, Leo 97
Anderson, Sir John *99*, *177*
Angel, SS (previously *River Clyde*) 46, *76*
Anglo-Irish Treaty 68, 75
Anschluss, Austria 90
Asquith, Herbert H 30, 34, 47, 54
Atlantic Charter 112–14
Attlee, Clement 98, *99*, 182, 185, 187, 205
Augusta, USS 112
Australian Infantry Battalion, 21st *49*
Axis forces, North Africa 128, 132, 136, 139

B

Baldwin, Stanley 76, 79, 85, 87
Balfour, Arthur 30, 34, 35
Balfour Declaration 75
Barnard Castle infantry school, Co Durham *137*
Battle of Britain 103, 105
BBC (British Broadcasting Corporation)
  100 Greatest Britons poll 6
  broadcasts 11, 122, *124*, 193, 201
Beaton, Cecil *101*
Beaverbrook, Lord *99*, 190
Belfast, HMS 152
Belgium *40*, 43, 46, 47, *130*, 159
Bengal famine 128, 132
Beveridge, William 187
Bevin, Ernest 98, *99*, *177*
'Big Three' conferences *142*, *143*, 146, 162, *166*, 168, 182, *185*
'Billy the goat' (mascot) *111*
Bishop, Lieutenant Colonel Alec 105, 108
Blenheim Palace, Oxfordshire 14, 30
Blitz, the 105, *109*, 112, *121*
'Blood, toil, tears and sweat' speech 100, *105*
Boer War (1899–1902) *20*, 22, *22*, 24, 28, 30
Bolshevism 64, 132
  see also communism
Britain
  air raids on 103, 105, *109*, 112, *121*
  appeasement policy 87–90, 94, 97, 98, 100
  declares war on Germany (1939) 94, 124
  defence spending 78–9, 87
  Dunkirk evacuation 100
  Gold Standard 76
  and Greece 159, 162
  industrial strikes 34–5, 37, *76*, 78
  Italian campaign 139
  North African campaign 128, 132, 136, 139
  'Phoney War' 94, 98
  propaganda posters *10*, *105*, *131*, *144*, *158*
  relationship with US 112, 129, 132, 193
  Siege of Sydney Street 35–7, *37*
  social reforms post-1945 185–7, 193–4
  VE Day 172, *175*, *176*, *177*, 178–9
  women's suffrage *28*, *32*, 34, 60–1
British Army
  Eighth Army 132, *135*, 136, 139, *160*
  4th Hussars *14*, 19, *20*, 139
  Royal Welch Fusiliers *111*
  Scots Guards 37, 47, *49*, 205
  21st Army Group *152*, 169
British Gazette 78
Brooke, Sir Alan *174*
Brunswick School, Hove 14
Buckingham Palace, London *175*, 178
Bulgaria 159
bulldog mascots *8*, *147*
Burma 128

C

Cabinet rooms, Downing Street *101*, *176*
Cabinet War Rooms (CWR)
  No 10 Annexe 105, 106, 108, *119*
  Remington typewriters *113*
  rooms 94, *114*
  War Cabinet meetings *99*, 100, 105, 112, *117*
Cadogan, Alexander *166*
Cairo conferences *70*, 139
Campbell-Bannerman, Sir Henry 30
Canada 112, 128, *129*, 139, *141*
Canford Cliffs, Poole *102*
Carson, Sir Edward 68
Casablanca Conference *138*, 139
Central Hall, Westminster speech *57*
Chamberlain, Neville 87, *89*, 90, 94, 97, 98
Chanak Crisis, Dardanelles 75
Chartwell house, Kent 76, 85, 190, *200*
Chiang Kai-shek 139
Churchill, Clementine (née Hozier)
  children 75–6, *122*, *200*
  duties in wars 47, 60, 110, *121*, 169
  receives Nobel Prize for Churchill 195
  Second World War 30, *31*, 169, *193*
  at State Funeral 205, 206
  travels with Churchill *70*, 82, *120*, 146

VE Day 178
and women's suffrage 34
Churchill College, Cambridge 206
Churchill, Diana 34, 82, *200*, 206
Churchill family *200*, 205, 206
Churchill, Lady Gwendoline (née Bertie) 83
Churchill, Jack 206
Churchill, Jeanette 'Jennie', Lady (née Jerome) 14, *18*, 24, 75
Churchill, John Spencer *see* Spencer-Churchill, John, 7th Duke of Marlborough
Churchill, Marigold 75
Churchill, Mary (later Soames) 76, *122*
Churchill, Captain Randolph *139*, *200*, 201
Churchill, Lord Randolph 14, 16, *18*, 19, 28, 201
Churchill tanks *158*
Churchill, Winston
   character and image
      accusations of heavy-handedness 34–7, 46–7, 64, 68, 75, 168–9
      boosts morale 60, *102*, 105, *110*, *111*, 132, 169
      bulldog mascots *8*, *147*
      'Churchilliana' *40*, *206*, *208*
      cigar and hat 6, *8*, *64*, *161*
      portraits *6*, *16*, *28*, *31*, *101*
      posters *10*, *105*, *130*, *131*, *144*, *158*, *187*
      reputation 51, 54, 75, 105, 187, 198
      statues and busts 75, 193, *193*, 206
      'V' sign 122, *124*, 206
   health problems
      accidents 83, 85, 198
      heart 128, *129*, 146
      pneumonia 139, *144*, 198
      strokes 190, 193, 194–5, 201
   hobbies and leisure
      holidays 76, 144, 146, 198, 201
      painting *82*, 83, 85
   military career *14*, 19–21, *20*, *40*, 47, *51*
   personal life
      childhood and education 14–19, *14*, *16*, *18*
      marriage to Clementine 30, *31*, *120*
      children 75–6, *122*, *139*, *200*
      homes 14, 30, 76, 85, 190, *200*
      finances 28, 76, 82, 189–90, *193*
      becomes 'Sir Winston' 194
      death 201
      funeral and burial *198*, 201–6, *203*, *204*
   political career
      'Big Three' conferences *142*, *143*, 146, *162*, *166*, 168, 182, *185*
      Chancellor of the Exchequer 76–9
      D-Day 152–9, *152*, *154*, *156*
      First Lord of the Admiralty 37, 40–3, *42*, 46–7, *49*, 68, *90*, 94
      Home Secretary 34, 35–7, *67*
      Liberal Party 30, *31*, 34, 35, 37, 76
      loses General Election (1945) 182, *183*, 185, *187*
      Minister of Munitions *50*, *57*, 60, 98
      MP 21, 24, 28–30, *28*, 76, 79, 193, 198
      Prime Minister *94*, 98–100, *99*, *101*, *174*, *176*, 193–4
      receives US citizenship 201
      Secretary of State for the Colonies *70*, 75
      Secretary of State for War and Air 64–8, *64*, *66*, *67*
   speeches
      'Blood, toil, tears and sweat' 100, *105*
      at Central Hall *57*
      at Empire Theatre *16*
      'End of the beginning' 136, 139
      'The Few' *10*, 103
      'Finest hour' 103
      'Sinews of Peace' 187–9, *189*
      'Some chicken, some neck!' 128, *129*
      US Congress *123*
      US lecture tours 28, 82–5, *85*
      'We shall fight on the beaches' 100, 103, *144*
   views
      British Empire 8, 11, 75, 79, 193
      communism 64, 132, 187, 189, 190
      Hitler and Nazism 87, *89*, 94, 128, 190
      Ireland 68, 75
      Royal Family 85
      socialism 30, 64, 76, 98, 132
      women's suffrage *28*, 34, 60–1
      Zionism 8, 75
   as writer
      A History of the English-Speaking Peoples 195, *198*
      journalism 19, 22, *22*, 28, 78, 82, 83
      Lord Randolph Churchill 30
      Nobel Prize for Literature 195
      The River War: an Historical Account of the Reconquest of the Soudan 21
      Savrola 82
      The Second World War 28, 82, 195
      The Story of the Malakand Field Force 19
      The World Crisis 76, 82
Ciano, Count Galeazzo *89*
cigar, La Corona *8*
Clemenceau, Georges *64*
Clerical Tythes Bill 21
Cold War 189
Collins, Michael 68
Colt Government (M1911) pistol *49*
Commission of Enquiry, Dardanelles affair 46, 54
Commons, House of 30, 54, 87, 97, 100, 103, 198
communism 64, 132, 187, 189, 190
Conservative Party
   appeasement policy 87–90, 94, 97, 100
   Churchill leaves 30, 34
   Churchill returns to 76
   coalition governments 47, 64
   general elections 64, 75, 79, 85, 187, 193
   Oldham constituency 21, 24, 28–30, *28*
   social policies 21, 187, 193–4
   Woodford constituency 193, 198
Consolidated Liberator B 'Winnie' (bomber) *8*
Coronation of Queen Elizabeth II 194
Council of Europe meeting, Strasbourg 190
Coventry Cathedral, bombing of *109*
Crewe, Earl and Countess of 30
Cripps, Sir Stafford *99*, 185
Cromwell, Oliver, quote 97
Cuba 19
Cunningham, Sir Andrew *174*
CWR *see* Cabinet War Rooms (CWR)
Czechoslovakia 90, 94, *105*

D

D-Day 152–9, *152, 154, 156*
Daily Graphic 19
Daily Mail 82, 83
Daladier, Edouard *89*
Dardanelles campaign 46–7, *46, 49,* 54
de Gaulle, General Charles 139, *149, 162,* 205
de Laveleye, Victor 122
Dempsey, Lieutenant General Sir Miles *152, 154*
Denmark, invasion of 94
Dewsnap, Dan 22
Doenitz, Grand Admiral Karl 172
Downing Street *see* No 10 Downing Street
Dresden, Germany, bombing of 168–9
Duke of York, HMS *122*
Dunkirk evacuation 100

E

Eastern Europe (post-1945) 159, 162, 168, 182, 189
Eccleston Square, London 30, 34
Eden, Anthony 99, *166,* 182, 193, 194, 195, 205
Edward, Prince of Wales (later King Edward VII) 14
Edward VIII, King (previously Edward, Prince of Wales) *67,* 85, *86*
Egypt *70, 135,* 136, 139, 141, *165,* 193
Eisenhower, General Dwight D *128,* 152, 193, 205
El Alamein, Battle of (1942) *135,* 136
ELAS (Greek People's Liberation Army) 159, 162
elections, general
    to 1918 24, 34, 64
    to 1935 75, 76, 79, 85
    from 1945 182, *183,* 185–7, 193, 198
Elgin, Lord 30
Elizabeth II, Queen 194, 201, 205, 206
Empire Theatre of Varieties, London speech 16
Enchantress, HMS 40, 43
'End of the beginning' speech 136, 139
Enterprise, HMS 156, 159
Epping constituency 76, 79, 85
Epstein, Jacob *193*
Everest, Elizabeth 14

F

fascism *89,* 139
'Few, The' speech *10,* 103
'Finest hour' speech 103
First World War
    Armistice 64
    Dardanelles campaign 46–7, *46, 49*
    Royal Naval Division (RND) 43, 46
    technology 43
    Western Front *40,* 43, 47, *49,* 51, *51,* 60
    Westminster memorial service *68*
Fisher, Lord, First Sea Lord 47
France
    Armistice Day (1944) *162*
    Dunkirk evacuation 100
    Foreign Office, Paris *50*
    Grande Place, Lille *59*
    holidays 76, 198
    Normandy 152–9, *152, 154, 156*
    Paris Peace Conference (1919–1920) *64*
    Western Front *40,* 43, 47, *49,* 51, *51,* 60
Free French forces 139, *162*
Free Trade policies 30
French Army, XXXIII Corps *51*
French Division, 29th *40*

G

Gallipoli 47, *49,* 76
Gandhi, Mohandas 'Mahatma' 8
Gaulle, Charles de *see* de Gaulle, General Charles
General Strike *76,* 78
George, David Lloyd *see* Lloyd George, David
George V, King 85
George VI, King 146, 152, 156
Germany
    Allied Rhine crossings *171,* 172, *174*
    Dresden bombing 168–9
    invades Europe 87, 90, 94, 97, 100
    Kristallnacht 87
    Luftwaffe 87, 103, 105
    Munich Agreement *89*
    Nazi-Soviet Pact 90
    North African campaign 128, 132, *135,* 136, 139
    Potsdam Conference 182, *185*
    zones post-1945 182
'Germany First' principle 129
Gneisenau (cruiser) 128
Gold Standard 76
Goldsworthy, Lieutenant Frank 114, 122
Government of India Act (1935) 87
Greece 159, 162, *164*
Greenwood, Arthur 98
Guildhall, London, bombing *121*

H

Halifax, Lord 98, 100
Harmsworth, Alfred, 1st Viscount Northcliffe *50*
Harriman, Averell *166*
Harris, Air Chief Marshal Sir Arthur 169
Harrow School, London *17*
health *see* Churchill, Winston: health problems
History of the English-Speaking Peoples, A (Churchill) 195, *198*
Hitler, Adolf 87–90, *89,* 94, 100, 103, 128, *131,* 172
Hollis, Major General L C Hollis *174*
Holocaust 87, 168
Home Rule Bill, Ireland (1912) 68
Hopkins, Harry 112
Howard, John 22
I bin-Al Hussein, Abdullah, Emir of Transjordan *70*

I

India
    Bengal famine 128, 132
    independence 79, 87
    4th Hussars *14,* 19, *20, 139*
industrial strikes 34–5, 37, *76,* 78
IRA *see* Irish Republican Army (IRA)
Iran *142, 143,* 146
Iraq 64, 68, *70*
Ireland 14, 68, 75, *75*
Irish Republican Army (IRA) 68, 75

'Iron Curtain' speech 187–9, *189*
Ismay, General Sir Hastings ('Pug') 108, 112, *174*
Italy 87–8, 139, *160*, *162*

J
Jaffa riots, Palestine 75
Japan 124, 128, 132, 169, 182, 187
Jewish people 8, 75, 87, 168
Juliana, Queen of Netherlands *182*

K
Kaplan, Samuel *8*
Kennedy, President John F 201
Keyes, Sir Roger *96*, 97
Keynes, John Maynard 76
Kitchener, Lord 19
Kristallnacht, Germany 87

L
Labour Party
    general election wins 76, 79, 182, 185, 193
    policies 35, 187
    War Cabinet 97, 98–100, *99*
Lambert, George 46
Lancers, 21st 19, 21
League of Nations mandates 68, 75
Leese, Lieutenant General Sir Oliver *160*
Leigh, Lance Corporal *8*
Lend-Lease Act 112
Lennox Hill Hospital, New York 83, *85*
letters home 54, 97–8, 124, 182, 185, 189
Liberal Party 30, *31*, 34, 35, 37, 76
Libya 132, 139
Lindemann, Professor Frederick 'The Prof' *96*, 98
Liverpool docks protests (1911) 37
Lloyd George, David 34, 54, 60, 64, *64*, 75
Lockheed Lodestar aircraft *135*
London, air raids on 103, 105, 112, *121*
London Transport poster *144*
Lord Nelson, HMS 40, 43
Lord Randolph Churchill (Churchill) 30
Lords, House of 34
Luftwaffe 87, 103, 105

M
MacDonald, Ramsay 76, 79
Macmillan, Harold 193–4, 198, 205
Malakand Field Force, India 19
Malaya 124, 128, 193
Malta Conference 159
Manchester North-West constituency 30
Mansion House speech 136, 139
Marsh, Edward 'Eddie' *59*
Mau Mau uprising, British Kenya 193
Menzies, Robert 205
Middle East 64, *70*, 75, *142*, *143*, 146, *165*
Molotov, Vyacheslav *99*, 132, *166*
Monte Carlo *193*, 198
Montgomery, Field Marshal Bernard
    Chief of Staff of 47th Division *59*
    Commander of 21st Army Group *152*, *154*, *155*, 156, 169, 172
    Commander of Eighth Army *135*, 136
    relationship with Churchill 182, 198, 201, 205
Moore, Major General Cecil *161*
Morning Post 22
Morocco 128, *138*, 139, *144*, 146, *149*
Morrison, Herbert *99*, *177*
Moscow Conference (1942) 132, *133*, 136
Moscow Conference (1944) 159, 162
Mountbatten, Lord 201, 205
Mulberry Harbours 152, *156*
Munich Agreement *89*
Mussolini, Benito *89*, 100, 139, 172

N
Narvik, Battle of 97
Nasser, Colonel 193
navy *see* Royal Navy
Nazi-Soviet Pact 90
Netherlands, the *182*
No 10 Annexe 105, 108, 112
No 10 Downing Street *101*, *174*, *176*, *203*
    see also Cabinet War Rooms (CWR)
Nobel Prize for Literature (Churchill) 195
Normandy 152–9, *152*, *154*, *156*
North African campaigns 128, 132, *135*, 136, *139*
Norway, invasion of 94, 97

O
Oldham constituency 21, 24, 28–30, *28*
Omdurman, Battle of 19, 21
Onassis, Aristotle 198
Operation 'Fortitude' 152
Operation 'Hope Not' (funeral plans) 201–5
Operation 'Overlord' 152
Operation 'Torch' 128, 132
Ottawa House of Commons, Canada speech 128, *129*

P
Paget, General Sir Bernard *137*
Palestine 75, 87
Pankhurst, Christabel *28*
Paris Peace Conference *64*
Pearl Harbor 124
'percentages agreement' 159, 162
Pershing, General John *67*
'Phoney War' 94, 98
Poland *25*, 90, 146, 168
Pond, Major James 28
Portal, Air Chief Marshal Sir Charles *174*
Portuguese East Africa 22
Potsdam Conference 182, *185*
Prince of Wales, HMS 114, 124
propaganda posters *10*, *105*, *130*, *131*, *144*, *158*, *187*

Q
Quebec Conference (1944) 159

R
RAF *see* Royal Air Force (RAF)
Realpolitik 133
Red Cross, Aid to Russia Fund 169

Remington typewriters, CWR *113*
Renown, HMS *141*
Representation of the People Act 60–1
Repulse, HMS 124
Rhead, Lieutenant Commander E B 156, 159
Rhine crossings, Germany *171, 172, 174*
RIC *see* Royal Irish Constabulary (RIC) ['Black and Tans']
River Clyde, SS (later *Angel*) *46, 76*
River Plate, Battle of 94
River War: an Historical Account of the Reconquest of the Soudan, The (Churchill) 21
RND (Royal Naval Division) 43, 46
Roberts-Jones, Ivor 206
Robertson, Field Marshal Sir William *66*
Rogers, Herman and Katherine *86*
Romania 159
Roosevelt, President Franklin D
    Atlantic Charter 112, 114
    'Big Three' conferences *142, 143*, 146, 162, *166*, 168, 182, *185*
    Casablanca Conference *138*, 139
    death 182
    Quebec Conference (1944) 159
    relationship with Churchill 112, 182, 193
    Washington 'Arcadia' Conference *122, 123*, 128
Royal Air Force (RAF) *10*, 64, 103–5
Royal Artillery Experimental Unit, Shoeburyness *170*
Royal Family 85, *86, 175*, 178, 194
    see also specific monarchs
Royal Irish Constabulary (RIC) ['Black and Tans'] 68, *75*
Royal Naval Air Service 43
Royal Navy 37, 40–3, *42*, 47, 68, 128
Rushbury, Henry, sketch *57*
Russia 64, *70*, 169
    see also Soviet Union
Russian Latvian siege, London 35–7, *37*

S
Salisbury, Frank O *6*
Salisbury, Lord 19
Sandhurst College, Berks 16
Sandys family *200*
Saud, King of Saudi Arabia *165*
Savrola (Churchill) 82
Scharnhorst (cruiser) 128
Scotland *57, 104, 141*
Scott, Peter 156, 159
Second Front 132, 136, 139, 146, 152
Second World War
    Allied invasion of Italy 162
    Armistice France (1944) *162*
    battles 94, 97, 103–5, *135*, 136
    'Big Three' conferences *142, 143*, 146, 162, *166*, 168, 182, *185*
    the Blitz 105, 109, 112, *121*
    Dresden bombings 168–9
    Dunkirk evacuation 100
    Normandy and D-Day 152–9, *152, 154, 156*
    North African campaign 128, 132, 136, 139
    Pearl Harbor 124
    technological advancements 43, 60, 152, *156*
    VE Day 172, *175, 176, 177*, 178–9
Second World War, The (Churchill) 28, 82, 195, *198*

Sheridan, Clare *75*
Sherman tanks 132
Short-Summer Pusher Biplane T2 *42*
Siege of Sydney Street, London 35, *37*
Simonds, Lieutenant General Guy *152*
Simpson, Wallis 85, *86*
'Sinews of Peace' speech 187–9, *189*
Singapore 128, 132
Sinn Fein 68
Soames family *200*
social reforms post-1945 185–7, 193–4
socialism 30, 64, 76, 98, 132
'Some chicken, some neck!' speech 128, *129*
South Africa 20, 22, *22*, 24, 28, 30
Southern Railways' locomotive 34051 (funeral train) 206
Soviet Union
    Battle of Stalingrad 136
    and Eastern Europe (post-1945) 159, 162, 168, 182, 189
    gulags 168
    joins Allies 113
    Moscow Conference (1942) 132, *133*, 136
    Moscow Conference (1944) 159, 162
    Nazi-Soviet Pact (1939) 90
    Second Front 132, 136, 139, 146, 152
    Sword of Stalingrad *142*, 146
    see also Russia
Spanish Civil War 87
Spencer-Churchill, John, 7th Duke of Marlborough *14*, 68
Spion Kop, Battle of 24
St George's Preparatory School, Hove 14
St Martin's Church, Bladon 201, 206
St Paul's Cathedral, London *204*, 205
Stalin, Joseph
    'Big Three' conferences *142, 143*, 146, 162, *166*, 168, 182, *185*
    Moscow conferences 132, *133*, 136, 159, 162
    'percentages agreement' 159, 162
    and Poland 168
    receives Sword of Stalingrad 146
    visit from Clementine Churchill 169
statues and busts *75, 193*, 206
Stettinius, Edward *166*
Story of the Malakand Field Force, The (Churchill) 19
Sudan 19, 21
Suez Crisis 193
suffrage for women *28, 31*, 34, 60–1
Sword of Stalingrad *142*, 146

T
Tehran Conference *142, 143*, 146
Thompson, Commander 156, 159
Thompson 'Tommy' submachine gun *128*
Trades Union Congress (TUC) 78
Transatlantic Telephone Room, CWR *114*
Transjordan *70*, 75
Truman, President Harry S 169, 182, *185*, 187, 193
TUC *see* Trades Union Congress (TUC)
Tudor, Lieutenant General Hugh 68
Tunisia 139, 146
Turkey 46–7, *46*, 68, 75

U

United Kingdom *see* Britain
United Nations, birth of 114, 168
United States (US)
    Atlantic Charter 112, 114
    citizenship of 201
    lecture tours in 28, 82–3, *84*
    Pearl Harbor 124
    relationship with Britain 112, 129, 132, 193
    Washington 'Arcadia' Conference *122, 123*, 128
    Westminster College, Fulton speech 187–9
USSR *see* Soviet Union

V

'V' for Victory gesture 122, *124, 206*
V2 rockets 112
VE Day 172, *175, 176, 177*, 178–9
Versailles, Treaty of 90
Vesey, General Sir Ivo 51
Vickers Maxim machine gun *20*
Victor Emmanuel III, King of Italy 139
Villa Lou Viel, Cannes *86*
Visitors book, CWR *114*
Voroshilov, Marshal Kliment *142*

W

Wales, Tonypandy riots 34
Wall Street Crash 82, 190
War Cabinet 94, 98–100, *99*, 105, 114, *117*
    see also Cabinet War Rooms (CWR)
War of Independence, Ireland 68
Washington 'Arcadia' Conference *122, 123*, 128
Wavell, Lord, Viceroy of India 132
'We shall fight on the beaches' speech 100, 103, *144*
Webley Wilkinson pistol *21*
Western Front *40*, 43, 47, *49*, 51–4, *51*, 60
Westminster Abbey, London *68*, 76
Westminster College, US speech 187–9
Westminster Hall, London 205
White anti-Bolshevik forces 64, *70*
Wildman-Lushington, Lieutenant Gilbert *42*
Wilkinson, Norman, *The Base Camp, Cape Helles, Under Shell Fire 46*
Wilson, Field Marshal Sir Henry 75
Winston Churchill (funeral engine) 206
Women's Social and Political Union (WSPU) *28*
women's suffrage *28, 32*, 34, 60–1
Woodford constituency 193, 198
Woolton, Lord *177*
World Crisis, The (Churchill) 76
world wars *see* First World War; Second World War
WSPU *see* Women's Social and Political Union (WSPU)

Y

Yalta Conference 162, *166*, 168

Z

Zionism 8, 75